THE NATURAL CREATIVE PROCESS IN WRITING

A CORE WRITING AND EDITING HANDBOOK FOR EVERYONE

THE NATURAL CREATIVE PROCESS IN WRITING

A CORE WRITING AND EDITING HANDBOOK FOR EVERYONE

Russell de la Porte

Publisher
WriteArt
P O Box 30601, Tokai, 7966, Western Cape,
South Africa

website: www.writeart.com
email: info@writeart.com

In the event of copyright holders or any other
person noticing any infringements, errors or
omissions in this publication, these have been
unintended. If we are contacted about any such
occurrences, we will be pleased to rectify them as
soon as we can.

First published in 2014

ISBN–13: 978-1530866328
ISBN–10: 1530866324

Acknowledgements
Cover design, publication design, illustrations &
typesetting: Lorne McGregor, LSM Graphics Copy-
editing & proofreading: Tessa Smythe Indexing:
Sanet le Roux

I dedicate this book to all who are on a quest for illumination and self-knowledge. May the principles, techniques and tools described accompany you throughout your life; may you use them for your own, and your fellow human beings' development and enjoyment.

CONTENTS

ACKNOWLEDGEMENTS

Course participants and other clients

I would like thank my clients, including course participants, for their input and feedback, which have contributed to the making of this book.

Production team

I would also like to thank Tessa Smythe for her incisive input on all aspects of this book and for her commitment to the project as a whole. This included not only her diligent copy-editing, but also her advice, encouragement and support. Tessa's work was key to bringing this book into being.

My thanks also go to Lorne McGregor for his enthusiasm for, and commitment to this work. His creativity, openness and flexibility also played a key role in bringing it into physical and digital being.

Contractors, subcontractors and associates

The support of contractors, subcontractors and associates has contributed to creating the enabling environment in which this project was conceived and conveyed, and I thank you all for this.

Mentors and friends

I wish also to thank my mentors and friends – some of whom are my clients – for their support and constructive input, which assisted me to create this book. I will remind you, individually, over time, to ensure that you know who you are.

HANDBOOK GUIDE

A new way

The Natural Creative Process in Writing: A Core Writing and Editing Handbook for Everyone provides a novel approach to writing that synthesizes the creative process, mind states and brain modes. Its format and design through to its structure and use of language were chosen with your reading experience in mind.

This handbook gets to the the point directly, and hence, quickly. To achieve this, it is divided into the methodology and tools, and supplementary information (in the form of the three Addenda and the 'Glossary').

The 'Introduction' provides the theoretical framework, as well as previews and synopses of the stages of the natural creative process. It also lists the tools provided for writers in the stages.

The natural creative process moves through four stages: water (stage 1), air (stage 2), earth (stage 3) and fire (stage 4). A chapter is devoted to each stage, and identifying stage visuals on the first pages make for easy reference.

For readers who may need to supplement their knowledge of syntax and punctuation, the Addenda ('Addendum 1: Language structuring'; 'Addendum 2: Punctuation'; 'Addendum 3: Editing checklists') and the 'Glossary' cover these areas. These readers will benefit from reading the Addenda and the 'Glossary' before reading the language aspects of 'Stage 3 (air): Writing and revising' and 'Stage 4 (earth): Editing'.

'Possible paths' takes a look at the possibilities and directions open to you after having read this book.

The 'Contents' and the 'Index' provide you with effective ways of quickly navigating this handbook, enabling you to use it as a handy reference work for all of your writing tasks and projects. The methodology used can also be applied to all the other areas of your life, and the navigating tools will help you to use this handbook as a reference work in these areas too.

May you enjoy this exciting journey!

INTRODUCTION

The natural creative process

One of the needs that all humans experience is the need to create. We create throughout our lives, and we all participate in a creative process whenever we create something. Whether we are arranging a party for a child, planning to have a swimming pool installed, starting a new company, doing a painting, designing a logo – in other words, creating anything – we are participating in a creative process. This means that it is not only artistic people who work with the creative process in their lives: we all participate in creative processes in our lives.

So it makes sense that if the creative process is such a natural – elemental – part of our lives, coming to understand how it works will allow us to align ourselves with it. And aligning ourselves with the process will allow us to participate in it with greater ease.

In addition to everyone participating – usually unconsciously and with varying degrees of comfort – in the natural creative process, we all externalize our ideas and communications in order to get things done, in other words, to create. We use words and images, both spoken and recorded, to do this. Think, for example, of how you sketch something – with a rough drawing or in words – to capture an idea or to communicate it.

Even if you roughly sketched your idea in diagrams, at some point you would use words as well to accompany these. Therefore, a vital aspect of any project is the written word – writing. Think of any project, no matter how small, as an example of this. Let us take, for instance, stocking up with groceries or drawing up a daily task list: both involve externalizing our thoughts in the form of writing, in these cases a shopping list and a task list. So we see that the creative process and writing are important aspects of all of our daily lives.

For many of us, the objects that we create – or that we wish to create – are written objects. For some, these are works of fiction (short stories, novels, plays, poetry, and the like); for others, they are non-fiction (autobiographies, blogs, essays, theses, cookery books, to name just a few). Bear in mind that the distinction between fiction and non-fiction is hazy; the important thing is that whether we are writing fiction, non-fiction or a mixture of these, we will be participating in a creative process, and we will be using writing for two purposes: one, to externalize our thoughts and communications; two, to create our written objects – stories, letters, blogs, essays, among others. Hence, for writers, both the process of creating (the creative process) and the creation (our written objects) require writing.

The stages of the natural creative process

We know that there is a process involved in creating anything, and we shall call this the *natural creative process* or its shortened equivalent the *creative process*. The field of project management has identified four stages, or phases, in the creative process, which are the following:

- Stage 1: initiation
- Stage 2: planning
- Stage 3: execution
- Stage 4: closure

Each of these stages has distinct characteristics.

We can begin our study by assigning some characteristics to each stage (you may recognize these characteristics by thinking about your own projects, or creative processes; for example, the holiday you planned or the birthday party you arranged).

Characteristics of the stages of the natural creative process

Note that these may vary depending on the area of activity involved.

Stage 1: initiation

- Information gathering
- Brainstorming
- Sketches
- Consultations
- Discussions
- Storage of information gathered
- Research

Stage 2: planning

- Organizational structuring
- Product design
- Product or service structuring or modelling
- Resource assessment

Stage 3: execution

- Production
- Development
- Construction
- Assembly

Stage 4: closure

- Detailing
- Finishing
- Refining

With this background, we could propose alternative generic names for each of the stages.

Alternative generic names for the stages of the natural creative process

- Stage 1: generating
- Stage 2: structuring
- Stage 3: constructing
- Stage 4: finishing

We could add the following additional characteristics to the above stages.

Additional characteristics of the stages of the natural creative process

Stage 1: generating

- Apparent lack of momentum
- Embryonic
- Invisible
- Lack of clarity
- New life
- Non-material (idea form)
- Pneuma
- Signs of growth
- Unconscious
- Unformed

Stage 2: structuring

- Beginnings of structure
- Increased presence
- Increased visibility
- Increasing momentum
- Modelling
- Outline design

Stage 3: constructing

- Crude form
- Formative expression
- Increasing momentum
- Material
- Visible

Stage 4: finishing

- Concrete
- Conscious
- Directing
- Preparing for delivery and use
- Specific

The characteristics of each stage – outlined above – are similar in many respects to what the classical elements water, air, earth and fire symbolize.

Classical elements symbolizing the stages of the natural creative process

- Stage 1: water
- Stage 2: air
- Stage 3: earth
- Stage 4: fire

An advantage of associating the four stages of the creative process with the classical elements is that it allows us to quickly identify the developmental stages of our projects as a whole, or any aspect of our projects.

Next, we look at the underlying states of mind associated with each stage of the natural creative process.

States of mind associated with the stages of the natural creative process

Stage 1: water

- Maximum stress (most self-management required)

- Maximum understanding, patience and trust in the natural process required
- Light bulb ('aha') moments

Stage 2: air

- Stress starts to relieve as project/ideas/planning start to take tentative form
- Discovery/experimentation regarding how to implement realizations

Stage 3: earth

- Reduced stress as project gains momentum
- Evidence of progress rewards our patience/trust/commitment

Stage 4: fire

- Minimum stress (usually stress is now deadline related)
- Project has its own momentum (challenge now is to keep up with the project's momentum)
- Celebrations

Finally, the terms that we will be using for the stages of the creative process as they apply to writing are as follows:

Stage names of the natural creative process applied to writing

- Stage 1: generating and research
- Stage 2: organizing and outlining
- Stage 3: writing and revising
- Stage 4: editing

Mind and brain functioning

Left and right mind states in this book are symbolic. Research from the 1960s through to the 1980s predominantly associated functioning and mind states with the left and right brain hemispheres (known as *lateralization*). Later findings, however, suggest that large areas of the brain are simultaneously involved in most types of functioning. In this book, these approaches are synthesized, with 'left brain' and 'right brain' symbolizing particular states of mind and mind functioning that have been broadly mapped to brain modes and brain functioning. In broadly mapping mind states to brain modes, it is assumed that there is integration within and across the brain hemispheres that occurs in varying degrees for each stage of the natural creative process.

In this book, it is assumed that left-mind-state and right-mind-state – corresponding with left-brain-mode and right-brain-mode – dominance is a matter of disposition, but that choosing our attitude, and consequently, our state of mind – by using the self-management tools offered – will result in our selecting the brain modes that are appropriate to the particular stage of our projects.

Thus, stage-appropriate attitudes and behaviours predetermine and engage the stage-appropriate state of mind (or *mind state*), and this, in turn, engages the stage-appropriate brain modes, involving neuronal activity within and across the brain hemispheres.

Terminology and abbreviations

In this book, the following terms and abbreviations are used for the concepts discussed above.

R state stands for the state of mind corresponding with *R mode* (right-brain mode) that is engaged in Stage 1 of the natural creative process. It is also used to refer to right-mind-state dominance.

R-L state stands for the integrated state of mind corresponding with *R-L mode* (right-left-integrated brain mode) that is engaged in Stage 2 of the natural creative process.

L-R state stands for the integrated state of mind corresponding with *L-R mode* (left-right-integrated brain mode) that is engaged in Stage 3 of the natural creative process.

L state stands for the state of mind corresponding with *L mode* (left-brain mode) that is engaged in Stage 4 of the natural creative process. It is also used to refer to left-mind-state dominance.

Characteristics of states and modes

In this book, R-state (and corresponding R-mode) functioning is predominantly associated with *creating* and L-state (and corresponding L-mode) functioning is predominantly associated with *analyzing*. R state is associated with the characteristics of Stage 1 (water) and to a lesser extent Stage 2 (air); L state is associated with the characteristics of Stage 4 (fire) and to a lesser extent Stage 3 (earth).

Many of us have a predisposition for L-state or R-state dominance. Then there are those who are not naturally mind-state, and corresponding brain-mode, dominant. These people freely switch between mind states and are at ease in all states, effortlessly moving between, and using parts of, both brain hemispheres.

Some individuals are polarized in their belief that their disposition – that is, their nature, or inherent personal makeup (L-state dominance versus R-state dominance) – and, hence, way of being, is superior. L-state-dominant individuals may fear the discomfort and apparent loss of control of R-state functioning. On the other hand, R-state-dominant individuals may fear the constraints of time and space that are necessary to bring their projects to successful completion. Those who have experienced, and are thus familiar with, freely switching and integrating their thinking, and consequent brain activity, will be more at ease with stage-appropriate behaviour and functioning.

We will experience discomfort when we are in the stages of the creative process and states of mind that are not favoured by our disposition. However, with an understanding of the natural creative process and the stage-appropriate states of mind and corresponding brain modes, we will become more comfortable with ourselves in our natural creative processes and with others in theirs.

Understanding our disposition will allow us to manage our discomfort in the stages of the natural creative process where our predominant mind state and brain mode – and hence, attitudes and behaviours – are the cause of this. This understanding will also promote harmonious team functioning – through an understanding and acceptance of complementarity in our relationships – in our writing and publishing projects, among others.

In the section below, the attitudes of *acceptance* and *non-criticism* are assigned to R-state and R-L-state functioning – associated with Stage 1 (water) and Stage 2 (air) respectively; *judgement* and *criticism* are assigned to L-state and L-R-state functioning – associated with Stage 4 (fire) and Stage 3 (earth) respectively.

Natural creative process stages and associated attitudes, behaviours and mind states

Stage 1 (water): generating and research

R-state dominance

- Creative
- Synthetical
- Accepting (non-critical)

Stage 2 (air): organizing and outlining

R-L-state integration (combined functioning, with R-state dominance)

- Creative-analytical
- Predominance of an accepting, non-critical attitude
- Complemented by an analytical, judging, critical attitude

Stage 3 (earth): writing and revising

L-R-state integration (combined functioning, with L-state dominance)

- Analytical-creative
- Predominance of a judging, critical attitude
- Complemented by creative, accepting, non-critical attitude

Stage 4 (fire): editing

L-state dominance

- Analytical
- Judging (critical)

Typically, the time spent in each stage is not equal: it is more usual for up to 60% of the duration of the entire project to be spent in Stage 1 (water) – and for each subsequent stage to take up an incrementally reduced proportion of time. Furthermore, our projects will gain in momentum as we progress through the stages.

Self-management

Writing is a process – a natural creative process – with cycles occurring within cycles and progression and regression typifying the process. By assessing our writing projects, we can determine what overall stage they are in and what stage parts (for example, chapters or sections) are in. If necessary, we will need to return to a preceding stage of the development of our text or part of it.

The implication of this is that while generally there will be a sequential progression through the stages of the natural creative process, as detailed in this book, we will jump backwards to previous stages and forwards to subsequent stages throughout the process until our writing projects have been completed.

To assess what stage our writing projects are in, we need to be familiar with the stages; that is, we need to understand the characteristics of each stage. We also need to be able to recognize whether we are in L state or in R state, and whether or not the state that we are in is relevant to the current stage of our writing project. Therefore, it would be useful to return to the sections above, as and when required, in order to become familiar with the stages and states, and how these interact.

Being able to assess the stage that our projects are in, and which mind state we are in, is useless unless we apply this ability to managing ourselves in the stages and states. This process is known as self-management, and self-management implies intrapersonal communication – otherwise known as self-communication, self-talk or self-parenting. Intrapersonal communication can take the form of intervening monologue, writing, speaking aloud to ourselves, gesturing, and image-making (visual representations). The important thing, though, is to ensure that we are in the mind state that is appropriate to the stage of our writing project, and that we do not allow over-participation by either the L state or R state in a stage for which it is not equipped. An example of this would be to allow the L-state editor to become involved in the R-state generating and research (water) stage. This would result in ideas being criticized and possibly rejected before they have been given the opportunity to develop sufficiently. What might have seemed to the L state to be a 'bad' idea might have, at a later stage, developed into a highly relevant idea that might have provided an innovation or solution, the key to the success of the project. The L state's ill-equipped involvement at too early a stage would have resulted in a loss to the writer and to the world at large.

To prevent, for example, the critical L-state editor – a very necessary role, but at the appropriate stage – from becoming involved in the initiation or generating and research (water) stage, we need to be able to intervene. And to intervene, we need to be equipped with knowledge. The appropriate self-talk at this stage would be something along these lines:

'This is not the appropriate stage to be assessing ideas; this is the stage to be generating ideas. I will allow you, my L-state editor, to assess these ideas later on; for now, it's time to have fun, to experiment and to dream. I give myself full permission to relax and enjoy my imaginative, inventive, R-state self. I am loving this experience of the creative, day-dreaming, child-like aspect of myself.'

Just as in the example above where we used self-talk – a form of self-management – to reposition ourselves, facilitating a shift from L state to R state, so we can self-talk ourselves into action when enough generating and research have been done, and we need the groundedness of the L state to galvanize our project into action.

This ability to manage ourselves in the creative process would be further aided by an understanding of which mind state predominates our thinking and our actions. If most of my thinking and actions display the characteristics of L-state dominance, I will be less at ease in the water/generating and research stage. I will need to reassure myself with the knowledge that it is appropriate, safe and right to be acting the way I have chosen and to be using the tools that I know are appropriate to this stage. I could also reassure myself that the discomfort that I am experiencing will ease up as I move into the more familiar L state, which will become increasingly dominant as I move towards the fire/editing stage.

If, on the other hand, most of my thinking and actions display the characteristics of R-state dominance, I will be less at ease in the fire/editing stage. I will need to reassure myself that it is appropriate to be taking the actions and using the tools necessary at this stage of the process in order to reap the benefits of my creativity.

The following sections provide previews of each stage of the natural creative process in writing and the topics covered in each stage.

Stage previews

The following stage previews and the topics covered in each are discussed in greater detail in the chapters dedicated to each stage.

Stage 1 (water): generating and research

The generating and research (water) stage is an R-state-dominated stage. R-state dominance is characterized by a child-like attitude.

Words that characterize this stage and state are the following:

- Adventure
- Beauty
- Being
- Creativity
- Daydreaming
- Developing
- Entrepreneurship
- Excitement
- Experimentation
- Exploration
- Feminine
- Fun
- Generosity
- Imagination
- Indomitability
- Innovation
- Inquisitiveness
- Inspiration
- Playfulness
- Receptive
- Soft
- Vision

Consciously assuming a *receptive* attitude in the generating and research stage of your writing project will enable you to shift into R state. Doing this is the first step in managing yourself in your writing project.

For many of us, the attitude and behaviour proposed in the natural creative process method of writing runs counter to the training that we received at school, where we were told to start writing as soon as we were given our topic.

It is important to do the following during the receptive generating and research stage: look, explore, be, take walks in nature (nature is a good stimulus), observe, receive, record.

There should be no attempts at structuring our ideas and thoughts at this stage, as doing so would encourage greater – premature – L-state involvement, and this would come at the cost of our ability to generate ideas. However, we should be recording our ideas, by whatever means that suit us, including writing them down.

The topics covered in the generating and research stage are the following:

- Storing and retrieving methods
- Freewriting
- Informal interviews
- Brainstorming (lists, mind-maps)
- Analogies
- Heuristics
- Research
- Specialist interviews

Stage 2 (air): organizing and outlining

The organizing and outlining (air) stage is predominantly an R-state stage but with increasing integration with L state. The L-state influence starts to bring order and coherence to the child-like inventiveness that is characterized by R-state functioning. It is as though a wise and nurturing parent has noticed the ingenuity of the child and wishes to assist the child with its creation.

Words that describe this stage and state are the following:

- Appreciation
- Awe
- Direction
- Encouragement
- Gentleness
- Guidance
- Kindness
- Nurturing
- Orientation
- Planning
- Protection
- Structure

In the organizing and outlining stage, you will provisionally organize your gathered information and materials, as well as your recorded ideas and research. Then you will name and arrange your groups. Finally, you will create an outline from your group names. At this stage, details are not important, just grouping, arranging (organizing) and outlining.

To start thinking in too much detail at this point would mean that you have allowed too much L-state involvement, which would be inappropriate at this stage. The first two stages – generating and research, and organizing and outlining – are predominantly R-state stages. However, as previously mentioned, the second stage is the first of the two integrated-state stages that are in-between the minimally integrated first, generating and research (R-state), and fourth, editing (L-state), stages.

The topics covered in the organizing and outlining stage are the following:

- Envisioning outcomes and communication context (SPAMM: subject, purpose, audience, medium, message)
- Information grouping (using chosen storage and retrieval method)
- Outlining (using group labels)
- Outline types (chart, linear, concept maps for fiction)
- Types of arrangement (temporal, spatial, importance, cause and effect, comparison and contrast)

Stage 3 (earth): writing and revising

As with the organizing and outlining (air) stage, the writing and revising (earth) stage is an integrated-state (L-R state) stage, but with reduced R-state influence. The functioning during this and the subsequent (fire) stage is dominated by L state.

The L-state influence places increasing emphasis on order and coherence, yet is receptive to the child-like inventiveness of R state. It is as though a matter-of-fact adult has stepped in to ensure that there is sufficient detail which is appropriate and correct, that it is correctly sequenced and that the project is delivered on time.

Words that describe this stage and state are the following:

- Construction
- Diligence
- Economy
- Energy
- Logistics
- Performance
- Relevance
- Sequence

During this stage you will write your draft, adding detail to your outline. It is important to remember that in writing your draft there will be some R-state influence. Too much consideration for correctness will entail too much L-state influence, and this will prevent the unhindered flow and inspiration needed to *generate* your draft.

During your first and subsequent revisions, ensure that information is correctly sequenced. Revise again and again, if necessary, placing more emphasis on detail with each revision.

The topics covered in the writing and revising (earth) stage are the following:

- Structure of expository texts
- Style (manuals, guides and sheets)
- Tight writing guidelines
- Vibrant writing guidelines
- Writers' tools
- Getting feedback
- Language conventions

Stage 4 (fire): editing

The editing (fire) stage is an L-state-dominant stage, with a small amount of participation – when required – of R state. The L-state influence places ultimate emphasis on relevance, economy, effectiveness and quality. Where required, it calls on the creativity and inventiveness of the right brain.

It is as though a discerning parent has stepped in at the last minute to ensure that all goes according to plan, that nothing has been left undone and that, as a result, there will be no unmet expectations – or that delivery exceeds expectations.

16

Words that describe this stage and state are the following:

- Accuracy
- Achievement
- Active
- Appropriateness
- Conventions
- Correctness
- Delivery
- Detail
- Effectiveness
- Elegance
- Engagement
- Excellence
- Hard
- Masculine
- Polished
- Prudence
- Quality
- Results
- Style
- Timeliness
- User experience

Topics covered in the editing stage are the following:

- Workflow (macroediting, microediting, editing strategy)
- Revisiting SPAMM
- Revisiting style
- Editing checklists
- Reference works
- Appointing a copy-editor

The outcome of optimally participating in the natural creative process as it applies to writing will be a text that successfully performs one or more functions.

Just as all people have unique fingerprints, they all – whether experienced writers, or not – have a specific and highly individualized way of expressing themselves. And while the stages of the creative process can be identified and specified, people will draw on and express this process in a very individualistic way.

Why we write

One reason we write is to achieve a specific outcome. And to do this, we have to present our thoughts and feelings clearly and persuasively.

We also write to externalize our thoughts and feelings, and in so doing we objectify them, gaining distance and perspective. In the process, we learn about ourselves – our inner worlds – and our projects, and so we and they grow.

Writing allows us to express ourselves; it allows us to create, and to share beauty, truth and knowledge. But our writings also have the power to bring about change, to move people to action, and to allow them to experience themselves and their worlds in new ways.

Summary

The natural creative process moves through four stages, or phases. These stages recur in various areas of nature and human endeavour, such as in the project management life cycle and writing, among others. The stages represent a movement from unconsciousness to consciousness and from the non-material (ideas) to the material (end product). Based on the characteristics of the stages, they can be be symbolized by the four classical elements water, air, earth and fire.

When we create, we participate in the natural creative process. Our sharing of this process unites us with all of humankind, because the natural creative process is active in all of our lives. Yet it also reinforces our individuality, because we participate in natural creative processes for unique reasons and in unique ways.

STAGE 1 (WATER)

GENERATING AND RESEARCH

Introduction

During the early stages of initiating any project, it is important to ensure that you are in the appropriate state of mind for the stage. Doing this will induce increased activity in the areas of the brain (R mode during the water stage) necessary to sustain this state of mind.

The necessary state of mind for the generating and research (water) stage is one of receptivity and openness. In this state of receptivity and openness, your intuition will be heightened. If you feel attracted to a particular piece of information, explore it further. Do not question your intuition, for if you start to assess this natural impulse, you will be inviting increased L-state activity and, hence, L-mode activity. This will prematurely shift you into the next stage of the creative process – or, at worst, hinder your creativity in the first stage. However, if through effective self-management, you reserve this L-state activity for when it will be appropriate, the whole picture will start to become evident at a later stage; with hindsight, you will become aware of the synchronicity of events leading up to your understanding and consciousness of the whole.

If you allow yourself to function without a conscious awareness of the final result, that is, without knowing the outcome, if you consciously allow yourself, therefore, to be in alignment with the natural flow of life, to be in a state of not knowing everything, your creativity will be enhanced, and you will experience the inspiration and express the genius that is the result of assuming this attitude of receptivity and openness.

Many of us were told at school that we were to start writing as soon as we were given our topic. Those of us who appeared to be blankly staring into space as we naturally moved into a receptive-creative state of mind (R state, with resultant increased R-mode activity) were often accused of daydreaming – the stage-appropriate response – and told to get on with the job of writing.

As explained previously, this type of behaviour is often the result of a lack of understanding of the natural creative process and of natural disposition as determinants of our dominant mind state. But with this understanding, we are well positioned to manage ourselves and others in all of our individual and communal projects and activities. An important consequence of this understanding is an awareness of the benefits of complementarity in all areas of our lives.

In the 'Introduction', we looked at why we write, concluding that one of the reasons is to achieve specific outcomes. We do this by externalizing our thoughts using writing.

Now, you might ask what the use would be of recording, or writing about, your ideas – including your tentative goals and desired outcomes – if these may not be used or may well change. The answer is that it is the act of externalizing, expressing, or writing, that is important, as it is this act that crystallizes our thinking and moves us and our projects from the unknown, or unconscious, to the known, or conscious. Also, since our memories tend to move with time – and are better kept uncluttered to deal with what is current – it is useful to keep records of our thinking, and the products of our thinking, our experiences, and our interactions that have led to our current position. Having kept records of the process leading up to the present, we will, at least, have the benefit of choosing whether or not to access and use these in the future.

Storing and retrieving

Before you start to externalize, or record, your thoughts by writing, you will need to think about the means, or 'containers', that you will use to do this. This refers to deciding on the system you will use to record and store what you generate and gather in the generating and research (water), and subsequent stages of the natural creative process.

It would be useless to be writing about our writing – or externalizing (otherwise known as exteriorizing or objectifying) our ideas – if we did not have a system for storing, or collecting, these ideas for future reference. This section proposes possible systems.

These 'containers' should permit you to store information in a random manner, but should also allow you to access and structure this information at a later stage, should you decide to use the information generated and collected.

Three of these 'containers' are the following (they are described in more detail further on, along with how to use them):

- Journal, or notebook
- Cards
- Digital files

You may choose one of the above for generating information and storing the material you have collected, generated and researched, or you may combine them. Remember, though, that the emphasis is on choosing a system that most easily and comfortably allows you to record information and to retrieve it.

With this in mind, allow a system that suits you to evolve as you work with it. This could develop over a number of years, or you may find that it takes you very little time to find the system that works best for you. Try to make the collection and retrieval of information that is important to you an ongoing aspect of your writings.

Journal, or notebook

This section shows you how to use a journal, or notebook, to support your writing, be this fiction or non-fiction. You could use it for doing, recording or writing about the following:

- Feelings
- Goals
- Musings
- Narrative snippets
- Paragraph role checks
- Perceptions
- Photographs
- Poems
- Reflections
- Sketches
- Story outlines
- Story synopses
- Story themes
- Themes

Of course, you could use your journal in other ways, too. You could use it for, or to write about, the following:

- Aspirations
- Basis for your family memoir
- Basis for your autobiography
- Calculations
- Collages
- Decision-making exercises
- Drawings
- Dream lists or wish lists
- Events
- New ventures
- Plans
- Thinking tools

Buy a journal, or notebook, that is easy to carry around with you. Doing so will allow you to capture those unplanned-for moments of inspiration. But it would be useless to record these moments if you could not easily access them again. This section shows you how to structure your journal so that you can easily access your information in the future.

Divide your journal page into three sections – columns or rows. The first column or row could be roughly half of the page width or height, with the remaining two columns or rows each being a quarter of the page width or height. Thus your column widths or row heights would be roughly in the following ratio: 50:25:25.

In the left-hand column, or top row, record what you have observed – that is, what you have read, heard or seen – or your own initial writings, or musings. Remember to date each entry.

In the middle column or middle row, record your reactions to and reflections on what you have read, heard, seen or written. These could be feelings, ideas, examples or comments. Note that, if required, the middle column and the left column could be switched, with the middle column being for your observations and the left column being for your reactions and reflections. In other words, where you envisage that your reactions and reflections could take up more space than your observations, use the left column for this, but, if you switch patterns, mark this clearly. You could also use the reverse of your page for your observations, in which case the front page would have only two sections, your main section and your reference section, and the reverse of your page would have only one section (unless you decide to include a reference section – column or row – on this page too). Figure 1a, below, illustrates the column version of this system using the front page only, while Figure 1b, below, illustrates the version of this system that uses the front and reverse of the page.

Column 1 (main column): Observations, quotations, among others (notes)	Column 2: Reflections / Column 3: Short bibliographical (in-text) references, and cross-references (journal category index labels), in square brackets		
25 Feb 14 Today I was given my assignment topic.	Not sure where to start – I feel in the dark/ at sea. Water stage.		[Assignment topic] [Journey]
28 Feb 14 'Asteroids are also known as minor planets, or planetoids.'	Get names of better-known asteroids.		Smith, 2009: 10 [Quote]
28 Feb 14 Smith, J., 2009. The Lives of Asteroids. Brighton: Academia Press.			Smith, 2009 [Biblio-graphical entry]

Figure 1a: Journal page with three columns, front page only.

In the right-hand column, or bottom row – your reference column, or row – keep a careful record of the sources of your quotations and the relevant page numbers. Apart from the possibility of wanting to refer to these again, in academic writing you will need to include these as your short bibliographical (in-text) references and in your bibliography, or references section. (Other expository writing also sometimes requires short bibliographical (in-text) references and bibliographies.) Next to your entry, record the following short bibliographical information: the author's name, year of publication and page number, or numbers. The full bibliographical details – the author's name, the date of publication, the title of the book or article, the place of publication and the publisher, as well as the library shelf location number – should be recorded once in a stand-alone entry in your main column.

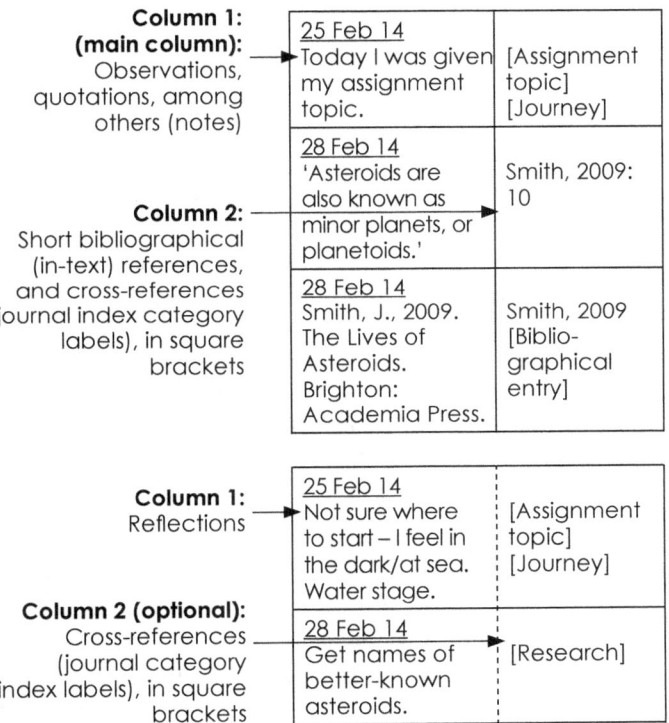

Column 1:
(main column):
Observations,
quotations, among
others (notes)

Column 2:
Short bibliographical
(in-text) references,
and cross-references
(journal index category
labels), in square
brackets

25 Feb 14 Today I was given my assignment topic.	[Assignment topic] [Journey]
28 Feb 14 'Asteroids are also known as minor planets, or planetoids.'	Smith, 2009: 10
28 Feb 14 Smith, J., 2009. The Lives of Asteroids. Brighton: Academia Press.	Smith, 2009 [Biblio-graphical entry]

Column 1:
Reflections

Column 2 (optional):
Cross-references
(journal category
index labels), in square
brackets

25 Feb 14 Not sure where to start – I feel in the dark/at sea. Water stage.	[Assignment topic] [Journey]
28 Feb 14 Get names of better-known asteroids.	[Research]

Figure 1b: (Top) Journal page with two columns on front page (Bottom) With one column (plus optional additional cross-reference for journal category index labels – see dashed line) on reverse page.

Your reference column could also be used for indexing and cross-referencing your journal entries. One way of doing this is to create different categories of entry. These could be, for example, the following:

- Bibliography
- Career
- Finance
- Health
- Recipes
- Recreation

- Reference
- Relationships
- Scenery
- Story ideas
- Studies

To create your category index, do the following. Starting on the last page of your journal, divide each page into the number of columns that will comfortably accommodate the date written in your handwriting. Next, list each category name, or keyword, at the top of a column. Thus, to use the category names above, the last column, starting on the last page of your journal would be headed 'Studies'; the second-last would be headed 'Story ideas'; the third-last, 'Scenery', and so on. Continue listing your categories on the reverse of this page.

When you have finished a journal entry, link it in your third referencing column, or row, to a category by writing down the name of the category to which it is linked. Distinguish these internal cross-references from other (external) references, though, by placing them, for example, within square brackets. After giving each entry one or more category names, record the date of your entry in the corresponding category columns at the back of your journal.

Category names →	Research	Journey	Bibliographical entry	Assignment topic
Entry dates →	28 Feb 14	25 Feb 14	28 Feb 14	25 Feb 14

Figure 2: Journal category index page at back of journal.

With your journal entries assigned to categories, and indexed at the end of your journal, you will easily be able to access the entries for each category, should you wish to do this.

You could also use your journal for any other generating strategies you use, such as, freewriting, mind-maps and questionnaires, cross-referencing them for later retrieval.

Bear in mind that the system proposed above is but one of many possibilities. You may find yourself customizing this system to suit yourself. This could include using separate journals for different life areas. For example, you may choose to have a separate study journal that you use for your academic writing. This journal could cover your writing topics, interviews, research, and meetings with your supervisor, among others.

Cards

This section shows you how to use cards to support your writing, also be this fiction or non-fiction. You could use them for writing about the same things as described above, for a journal, or notebook.

As with using a journal to record your ideas, observations, research and other matters relating to your writing, choose a card size that is easy to carry around with you, and that you feel comfortable using. Visit your local stationery shop to see what is on offer. And while you are there, check what storage systems are available for the card size that you choose. Since you will probably use many cards and holders in your writing projects, it would be wise to consider their prices, before you adopt this system.

The front of your cards corresponds with the first column, or row, of your journal. This is where you record your observations, ideas, insights, among others – remember to date each card – as well as your short bibliographical references. Divide your cards horizontally or vertically in two, in a ratio that suits you. Where you wish to record a reference, use the bottom half, or right or left side – depending on how you have decided to divide your card.

The reference recorded here is a shortened version equating to the short bibliographical (in-text) reference that you will use in your academic essay or thesis, or other expository writing. The shortened reference records the author's name, the year of publication, and the page numbers of the source text that you wish to quote, or cite.

Cards usually have a top margin on both their front and back sides, and these are useful for recording category names or keywords, as they allow you to access them without removing the cards.

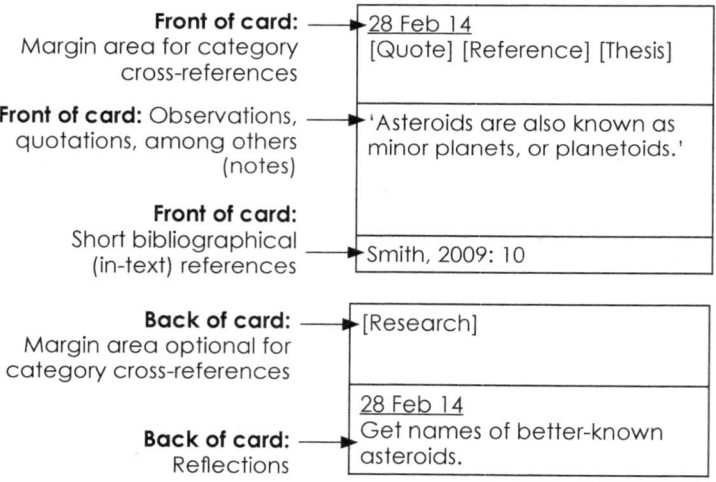

Front of card: Margin area for category cross-references — 28 Feb 14 [Quote] [Reference] [Thesis]

Front of card: Observations, quotations, among others (notes) — 'Asteroids are also known as minor planets, or planetoids.'

Front of card: Short bibliographical (in-text) references — Smith, 2009: 10

Back of card: Margin area optional for category cross-references — [Research]

Back of card: Reflections — 28 Feb 14 Get names of better-known asteroids.

Figure 3: (Top) Card with two rows on front of card for observations, notes, and the like, and short bibliographical (in-text) references (Bottom) Back of card for reflections, also using margin area for category cross-references.

The back of your cards corresponds with the second column, or row, of your journal. Here you record your observations about, reactions to, and reflections on what you have written.

As with the journal, you could use the front and back margin areas to write down the categories to which you feel a card belongs, that is, for cross-referencing your cards. Also as with the journal, these could be differentiated from your external references by placing them within square brackets.

There are many ways of filing your cards; you could file them in date order, or in the order of your most important, or primary, categories. You could also use colour-coding, for example, if this suits you better. If you wish to recategorize a card, you could type up and print out a new version of the category names, and then paste this over your previous version. You could also use file tabs, or labels, at the top of your cards for your category names, instead of, or together with, writing or pasting these in the top margin area of your cards.

Use one card per quotation or theme, and if you run out of space to write on a card, continue on one or more cards then staple them all together in the order in which you have written on them. As you will see further on, the reason for doing this is that when it comes to organizing your information, and outlining or structuring your text, you will be able do this by arranging your cards in the order in which you want the information in your text to be sequenced.

For each short bibliographical reference that you write in the reference section of your cards, you should write down the full bibliographical information on a separate card. Doing this will mean that you do not have to source this information at a later stage. As you will see further on, each bibliographical card will represent a separate entry in your bibliography or reference section.

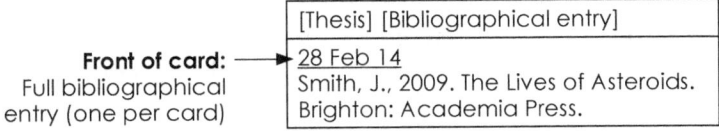

Front of card: ─────▶
Full bibliographical
entry (one per card)

| [Thesis] [Bibliographical entry] |
| 28 Feb 14 |
| Smith, J., 2009. The Lives of Asteroids. Brighton: Academia Press. |

Figure 4: Separate bibliography card (one per full biblio-graphical entry), with margin area for category cross-references and main area for full bibliographical details.

Again, as with the journal, it would be useful to create an index reflecting your category names or keywords. A primary index card could list all of your categories in the order in which they are filed, while a separate index card could list all of the entries for a category. Your index cards could be kept either at the front or back of your card container.

If your cards are filed in date order – as with your journal entries – you could give each category name its own index card. Divide the index card into columns, and list the dates of the entries that have been assigned the relevant category name.

Thesis	Research	Quote	Bibliographical entry
28 Feb 14	28 Feb 14	28 Feb 14	28 Feb 14

Category names →

Entry dates →

Figure 5: Category index card at front of card container.

In addition to the role it plays in indexing your cards, dating each entry is a useful practice because this will give you a sense of the stage of the process that you were in when you made the entry.

Digital files

If you prefer to make notes using digital files – with a hardware device such as a computer, mobile phone or tablet, among others – use the main sections outlined above for the journal and the card systems of making notes.

Use one section of your file for your ideas, quotations, observations, among others; another for your short bibliographical references; another for your reflections; and one for your category index labels. Also make sure that each entry is dated.

Give your files clear, descriptive names, and consider incorporating the date in your file name (your files will be listed alphanumerically from the left of the file name). Making one entry per file will allow for easy external referencing using your separate index file (see below) and the preview pane in your file management program, for example, Windows Explorer and its Apple and Linux equivalents.

File name: Topic_Record date_Title

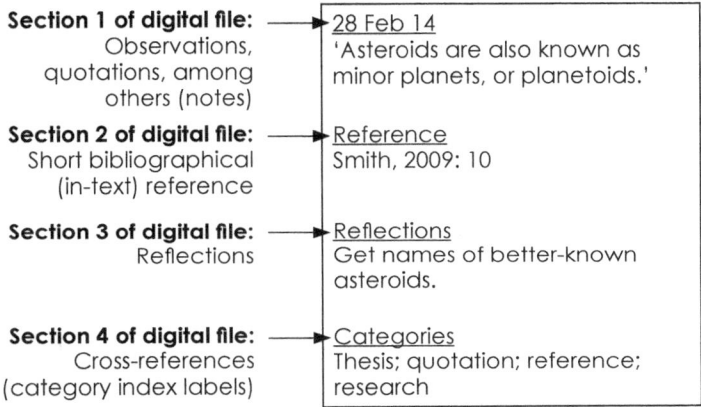

Section 1 of digital file: ──► 28 Feb 14
Observations,   'Asteroids are also known as
quotations, among   minor planets, or planetoids.'
others (notes)

Section 2 of digital file: ──► Reference
Short bibliographical   Smith, 2009: 10
(in-text) reference

Section 3 of digital file: ──► Reflections
Reflections   Get names of better-known
        asteroids.

Section 4 of digital file: ──► Categories
Cross-references   Thesis; quotation; reference;
(category index labels)   research

Figure 6: Main record file, with a section for observations, quotations, or other information; a reference section; a reflections section; and a category cross-references section.

Use a separate file for all of your full bibliographical entries for a particular text.

**File name: Topic_Record date_Surname_Initials_
Publication date**

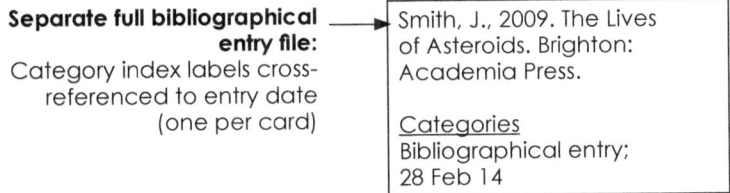

Separate full bibliographical ──► Smith, J., 2009. The Lives
entry file: of Asteroids. Brighton:
Category index labels cross-   Academia Press.
referenced to entry date
(one per card)   Categories
        Bibliographical entry;
        28 Feb 14

Figure 7: Separate bibliography file (one per full bibliographical entry), with category cross-references labels.

Also create a separate digital index file with hyperlinks to your files for a particular text. Your index file could include a brief description of the digital file to which it refers. It also could contain the category names listed in the reference sections of your digital files for a particular text.

	Date	Record opener/ Bibliographical entry	Reference	Hyperlink
Table (column) headings →	28 Feb 14	'Asteroids are also ...'	Smith, 2009: 10	File name: Topic_ Record date _Title
Records (rows) <	28 Feb 14	Bibliographical entry	Smith, 2009: 10	File name: Topic_ Record date_ Surname_ Initials_ Publication date

Figure 8: Digital index file with hyperlinks.

Using a database, spreadsheet or table in a word-processing file would be best for this exercise, as the tabular format will allow for greater flexibility when sorting your data entries, or records. (The database term for a column is *field;* for a row it is *record*: in doing this, you will have created a database.)

By using a file management program like Windows Explorer or My Computer, or the Apple, Linux or other operating system equivalents, you will be able to assign a title, tags, categories and summaries of your file contents without having to open your files. This is best done by viewing your files using your file preview pane. You will also be able to copy directly from your preview pane. This is useful when creating your outline, which is covered in the next (air) stage of the creative process. The technical aspects of file management programs are not dealt with here, but this information is available in the help files for the computer program you choose to use.

A final word on storing and retrieving

While there are many methods for storing and retrieving your information – only some of which have been proposed – the following are the most important aspects of this section:

Do:

- Record your ideas, insights, research and quotations; reflections on your ideas; short bibliographical (in-text) references; and full bibliographical information, among others.
- Have a way of storing the above information, but consider dividing it into a section for your ideas, quotations, observations, and the like; a section for your reflections on these; and a section for your references, short bibliographical (external) and cross-referencing (internal). The latter will be the basis for indexing your entries.
- Create an index or other way of retrieving your information so that you can easily locate what you are looking for.
- Ensure that your index or other way of retrieving your information is functional and sustainable. In this regard, consider whether you would be able to describe your system to someone else and whether that person could use your instructions to retrieve and replace information on your behalf.
- Customize, or individualize, the way that you store and retrieve your information so that it suits you.

With a system chosen for storing and retrieving your information, you are in a position to use the tools available for generating, researching and validating ideas, material, findings, quotations, and other content that can be used in your text.

The tools used to generate content for your text are described in more detail below – all involve writing, that is, externalizing your ideas using writing.

Generating

During the first (water) stage of the natural creative process, your emphasis should be on gathering information and speaking to people – if you are a student, this will include your supervisor. Go into a library or a bookstore and browse, collect brochures, take breaks, doodle, explore.

An important aspect of being receptive – the stage-appropriate attitude – is to consciously assign your project to your subconscious mind. You may have heard people saying 'I am going to sleep on it', and this means assigning a matter to their subconscious minds so that this part of their minds can work with it. Try to be aware of what specific issues you would like dealt with and what outcomes you would like to experience. If you are not clear on what these are, then be specific about expecting your subconscious mind to deliver clarity on what would be required for the project to progress further.

Once you have assigned to your subconscious mind whatever it is that you require it to work on, take breaks and indulge in recreation and play. Doing so implies trust that your subconscious mind will produce the required results – by going to work while you are at play or asleep – and it is your trust in this process that will allow your subconscious mind to do so.

The ability to trust in the power of your subconscious mind, in turn, follows an attitude of expectation and excitement. Therefore, be on the lookout for the resolution that you sought. This will synchronistically occur in what, without an awareness of the principle of synchronicity, might otherwise appear to be a series of unrelated coincidences. (Swiss psychiatrist Dr Carl Jung conceived this principle, which maintains that events are meaningfully related.)

When you have started to gain clarity – remember that this will be an ongoing process – on the direction that your writing project will take, you will be in a position to start more formal research, which is covered further on.

The next step in the natural creative process is to generate ideas for your content. The following sections outline techniques for shifting yourself into right-mind state/-brain mode, and for generating ideas.

Freewriting

One of the best tools we can use to shift ourselves into R state is freewriting. With pen or pencil and paper, or with keyboard and digital device, write or type whatever comes into your mind. As you do so, bear the following freewriting do's and don'ts in mind:

Do:

- Set yourself a target amount to write, or alternatively, a target period of time for writing.
- Keep your pen on the paper, or your hands on the keyboard.
- Write or type whatever comes into your mind.
- Keep up a good pace.
- Keep writing or typing without stopping until you have reached your target amount of, or time for writing.

Don't:

- Focus on your handwriting.
- Correct your spelling, syntax or grammar.
- Check for logic or sense.
- Attempt to steer your thoughts.
- Read what you have written – this keeps the critical L state from becoming active.

When you have finished writing or typing, you can choose to either retain what you have generated or destroy it. While your freewriting exercise may have generated ideas – which you may choose to retain, by storing your freewriting either as a whole or by just noting the important ideas, or destroy – the main purpose of the activity is to shift yourself into R state.

Brainstorming

One of the best tools we can use to generate ideas is brainstorming. As you do so, bear the following brainstorming do's and don'ts in mind:

Do:

- Write or type whatever ideas come into your mind, whether they seem 'sensible' or not.
- Focus on allowing previous ideas to generate other ideas.
- Use whatever system seems natural to you, for example, lists and mind-maps (see below for more information on these), among others.

Don't:

- Criticize, assess or analyze your ideas.
- Focus on the links or relationships between ideas.
- Attempt to structure your ideas.
- Use a brainstorming method that does not feel natural to you.

You can come back to the ideas you generate, at a later stage, in any of the mind states and creative process stages. Assessing your ideas will entail a move into the subsequent stages of the creative process, shifting you into a more analytical mind state, which will invite greater L-state/-mode participation. In these subsequent stages and mind state/brain modes, you will be in a far better position to assess your ideas. Attempting to do this too soon will prevent the natural flow that is characteristic of the generating and research (water) stage and the creative R state/mode.

The two main ways of brainstorming are lists and mind-maps, and these are described below.

Lists

When you enter items each on a new line, you are creating a list. This also applies to a brainstorming list. To start, simply write down each new idea on a new line. Do not number your lists, as this will entail structuring and will invite increased analytical, L-state/-mode participation, shifting you into the organizing and outlining (air) stage of the creative process. The result of this will be impeded generation and flow of ideas. Using a bullet for each new item could be an alternative to numbering, but this would be a duplication of the purpose for entering each new item on a new line, that is, to indicate that it is a separate, and distinct, item.

Mind-maps

With mind-maps, each new idea is represented by a graphical shape, for example, a circle or a square, which encloses the written idea. Where a previous idea has led to a subsequent idea, draw a line from it to the previously used shape, but do not focus on the links or relationships between ideas.

If you do not have an idea to write or type, simply draw a shape, and keep doing so until you have another idea. When this happens, either connect it to the idea that inspired it, or simply write or type it in one of the available shapes.

As with lists, do not focus on linking the unconnected shapes, as this will entail structuring and will invite increased analytical, L-state/-mode participation, shifting you into the organizing and outlining (air) stage of the creative process. The result of this will be impeded generation and flow of ideas.

When you have finished your mind-map, you can structure it. This will entail increased analytical, left-state/-mode participation, resulting in shifting you into the next creative process stage (air) and mind state (R-L state).

Analogies

When certain aspects of two things that would not normally be compared with each other are compared and contrasted, an analogy is being made. The comparison being made will be to something that is familiar. It could also be made to something with which it would not normally be compared. By linking the unfamiliar to the familiar, analogies are used to illustrate or teach, to provide a deeper understanding.

There are two basic types of analogy – whole analogies and part analogies – that can be used to generate ideas, and these are described below:

- Whole analogy: choose something or someone with which or with whom you can compare your idea.
- Part analogy: choose a part of something or someone with which or with whom you can compare your idea.

Now draw a table with two columns. In the first column, write all the similarities between what you are comparing; in the second column, write all of the differences.

Using either or both of the above analogy types, you could make new discoveries or arrive at a deeper understanding of the concept you are exploring or that you wish to impart or explain.

Heuristics

This generative process involves using speculation to guide discovery and learning through making inferences from general knowledge, trial-and-error experimentation, and non-scientific, rule-of-thumb, evaluation.

Heuristics is a quick way of generating ideas, or deepening our understanding of these, and of explaining them. One method involves choosing a concept, a topic, a desire, or a proposed project, among others, and questioning it.

In doing so, do not use reference works, such a dictionary or an encyclopaedia, because this more evaluative type of exercise will shift you into a subsequent – and currently inappropriate – stage, state and mode.

In using the heuristic method of generating ideas, bear the following do's and don'ts in mind:

Do:

- Set yourself specific questions – see ideas for questions below.
- Keep your pen on the paper or your hands on the keyboard.
- Write or type whatever comes into your mind.
- Keep up a good pace.
- Keep writing or typing without stopping until you have answered all the questions you have set yourself.

Don't:

- Focus on your handwriting.
- Correct your spelling, syntax or grammar.
- Check for logic or sense.
- Attempt to steer your thoughts.
- Read what you have written – this will keep the critical left-mind state from becoming active.

The following are some of the questions that you could use for your idea, topic or concept, among others:

- What are the beneficial aspects?
- What are the harmful aspects?
- What are the advantages?
- What are the disadvantages?
- Who or what will benefit?
- Who or what will suffer?

You could also do the following, but because they are more evaluative than the preceding generative activities, ensure that they are done towards the end of your generating activities and before you start your research.

- Define the concept.
- Write a glossary.
- Find synonyms.
- Find antonyms.
- List the components and subcomponents.
- Describe the relationships between the components.

Informal interviews

Informal interviews involve talking to colleagues, other students, lecturers, family members, your partner and anyone else with whom you feel comfortable discussing your ideas. Some of them may be familiar with your topic and others may not be, and their input could range from emotional support to specialist, or technical, input.

Research

The result of having generated provisional content for your text is that aspects of it will need to be verified, and some areas will be new and unexplored territory for you. Both of these scenarios will necessitate research, which can take many forms. Internet and library research are the two main forms, but we can also do specialist interviews, fieldwork and experiments. The important aspects of the first three of these – Internet research, library research, and specialist interviews – are discussed below.

Internet research

Internet research involves using an Internet browser, which is a computer program used to read and interpret the programming languages – or coding, for example, HTML (hypertext markup language) – that are used to write web pages and present these as regular text pages. Internet browsers, in turn, use search engines to locate the information that you type into their query bar.

Your ability to search the Internet for information will be greatly improved if you use wildcards in your searches. *Wildcards* are characters or groups of these that represent the information you are searching for. An example of a wildcard is the asterisk, which represents any other character in the same position as it is. Wildcards are not dealt with in detail here, but information is available on the Internet and in courses and books on Internet searching and wildcards.

A further aspect of searching on the Internet is using the specialized systems for storing and retrieving web pages that all web browsers have. These are known as *bookmarks,* though some browsers use different terms for these systems.

Use bookmarks for storing web pages that you feel are worth noting for future reference. As with wildcards, the technical aspects of bookmarking are not dealt with here, but this information is available in the help files of the browser that you choose to use. Remember, though, that your bookmarking system should work together with, or link up with, your journal, card or digital file system for storing and retrieving information. To do this, include the bookmark location of your sources wherever you have recorded bibliographical information, so that you can retrieve your online sources easily when you need them.

Library research

Guides for using public, academic and special libraries are often available online. These describe, among other things, the systems that are used for storing books and other materials, and the procedures involved in borrowing and returning items. Where they are not available online, the relevant librarian will be able to explain everything to you and may be able to give you a hardcopy version of the guide.

It would be worth your while to acquaint yourself with these systems and procedures, as well as to note the library shelf location number of your sources where you have recorded bibliographical information in your journal, cards or digital files, so that you can retrieve these easily when you need them.

Specialist interviews

Unlike the informal interviews you did while generating ideas, specialist interviews involve seeking the input of specialists in their fields or disciplines about a specific aspect of their work that relates to your topic.

Use your journal, cards or digital files to prepare for the interview, as well as to record responses during and after your interview. Remember to record the details of the interview where you usually record your bibliographical information.

Summary

During the generating and research (water) stage of the natural creative process, it is necessary to be in the stage-appropriate mind state and brain mode (R state/mode). This, in turn, is the result of adopting the appropriate attitudes (receptivity and openness) and behaviours (assigning your project to your subconscious mind, among others) for the first (water) stage of the creative process.

Three possible ways of storing and retrieving the information and materials generated are described. These are a journal, or notebook, cards and digital files.

The tools described for generating ideas and content are freewriting, brainstorming, analogies, heuristics, and informal interviews.

The research methods described are Internet research, library research and specialist interviews.

In the next stage – the organizing and outlining (air) stage – we will look at ways of organizing the information that you generated and researched. After organizing your information, you will be in a position to create an outline (or wireframe) for your draft text, which you will write in Stage 3, the writing and revising (earth) stage.

STAGE 2 (AIR)

ORGANIZING AND OUTLINING

Introduction

At the onset of the second (air) stage of the natural creative process, you will need to put yourself in the appropriate state of mind (R-L state) for this stage. Doing this will induce increased activity in the areas of the brain (right-brain mode with increased, though limited, left-brain integration) necessary to sustain this state of mind.

The necessary attitude for the organizing and outlining (air) stage is one of guiding and directing, that is, structuring and designing. During this stage, a formative – provisional – structure for your text will emerge. This will shape your draft text – sometimes referred to as your first draft. In this book, it is referred to as the *draft*, and subsequent, modified drafts are referred to as *revisions*.

Envisaged outcomes determine input

Envisaged outcomes entail viewing your message from beyond its delivery. Having done this, you will be in a position to set communication goals that are aimed at achieving your envisaged outcomes.

Up to this point, your emphasis will have been on what you wanted to say, or tell – your subject matter. At this point, though, you will need to start considering the context in which you will be communicating. This context encompasses what you wish to convey (subject), your intention in communicating (purpose), with whom you wish to communicate (audience), and the channel you wish to use to convey your message to your audience (medium). These factors will shape, and result in, the format of your communication or text (message). The reason you need to consider your subject, purpose, audience, medium and message (SPAMM) now, before organizing and outlining your draft, is that doing so may reveal gaps in your generated and researched information and material.

Considering your outcomes in terms of your SPAMM prior to this point, during the generating and research (water) stage, would have introduced too much structure, which could have impeded the free flow of your ideas and information.

So, for example, considering SPAMM for a university student could involve the following communication factors:

- Subject (research findings)
- Purpose (to report on findings)
- Audience (supervisor and peers)
- Medium (print, and published locally online)
- Message (form that the subject matter will take in writing – a thesis or dissertation)

From this point forward, you will need your SPAMM to become a guiding consideration when organizing, outlining and writing your draft, as well as when revising and editing your final draft. You will need to consider more consciously what (subject) you want to tell, why (purpose) you want to tell, who (audience) you want to tell, and how (medium) you are going to tell (message). These factors, in turn, will influence the content of your message and shape how it is packaged, that is, how it is written.

Grouping information

The following sections describe how to use the three note-taking methods introduced in 'Stage 1 (water)' – journal, or notebook, cards and digital files – to arrive at a provisional structure for your draft. Here you learn how to group information together using your chosen method, and how to label your groups of information. This involves using keywords and key phrases to characterize or summarize your information groups.

The group labels you use will later become provisional headings and subheadings in your outline, which could be expanded or altered to become final headings and subheadings – depending on your target publication's style requirements – see 'Stage 4 (fire)' – or they could be deleted in your final text. For some people, colour-coding is a favoured visual aid used to quickly and easily identify information that belongs together in one group, and identification using colour is an option, in addition to the group labels.

For all methods, your groups – identified by your group labels – will each represent one paragraph. Later, you will use outlines – also known as wireframes – to arrange your paragraphs. How you sequence your paragraphs will indicate the relationships between them.

Grouping information using a journal

In your journal, identify information that belongs in its own group. Label this above the beginning of the sentence where the new information group starts, or in the column or row that you have used for category names, or label in both places. If you want your labels to be easily distinguishable from the rest of your entries, you could use upper case (capitals) to do this, or you could place them within square brackets, or you could use both of these methods. As a visual aid, you could colour-code them, using coloured pencils or pens. Adopt the method that suits you best.

Grouping information using cards

To group the information recorded on your cards, sort through them and place those that belong together, because they deal with one topic, in their own group. If you come across a card that does not fit into any of the existing groups, place it on its own, as the start of a new group.

For each group, use a sticky note to make a group label, and place this on the top of each pile – or group – of cards.

Grouping information using digital files

As with your journal, identify information that belongs in its own group. Label this above the beginning of the sentence where the new information group starts, or where you have placed your category names, or label in both places. If you want your labels to be easily distinguishable from the rest of your entries, you could use upper case (capitals) to do this, or you could place them within square brackets, or you could use both of these methods. As a visual aid, you could colour-code them, using font colours or highlighting.

By using a file management program – like Windows Explorer or the Apple, Ubuntu or other operating system equivalents – you will be able to assign titles, tags, categories and summaries to some of your file types, and you could include your labels here.

If you have added your titles, tags, categories, summaries and labels to the column headings in your file management program, by sorting your files in title, tag, category, summary or label order with your preview pane showing, you will be able to view the information within your files (including your labels), in the order in which you want it arranged.

With an understanding of the different ways of grouping your information, you will be able to organize it to form a structural basis for your text.

Arranging information groups

Now that your information has been grouped, it needs to be arranged, to enable you to produce your outline. This is done in the ways described below, depending on the method you used for storing your information – journal, cards or digital files.

Many texts have headings comprising various levels, or hierarchies, of information. In arranging them, sometimes the first level or first order is indicated by a number without any decimal places; the second level or second order is indicated by one decimal place; the third level or third order is indicated by two decimal places; and so on. The system used to portray the hierarchical levels depends on the style – described in the writing and revising (earth) stage – applicable to your text. These levels and, hence, numbering systems, should be reflected in the numbering of your group labels – in your journal, on your piles of cards or in your digital files.

Arranging using a journal

Using a pencil (or coloured pencils, if this suits you), number your groups next to your group labels. Each group should have only one number assigned to it.

Choose a method for numbering subsidiary groups of information and use this method for your group labels in your journal.

Arranging with cards

Physically arrange your groups of cards into the correct sequence, and number your groups either by using another sticky note or by writing the number in pencil next to your group label. Each group should have only one number assigned to it.

Sometimes a group will appear to be different from, yet related to another group. This could mean that the group is a subsidiary group, and if this is the case, this relationship will be reflected in your text. Therefore, place related groups close to one another; that is, group your groups, and number accordingly, possibly using decimal places.

As with numbering related groups of information described for a journal, above, choose a method for numbering subsidiary groups of information, and use this method for labelling your groups of cards.

Arranging using digital files

As with numbering your group labels using a journal or cards, place a number next to your group labels in your digital files. Again, each group should have only one number assigned to it.

You could also place a number before your group labels in your file management program (remember to start numbering with a zero; so, for example, for the number *1*, use the digits *01*; otherwise, group *10* will follow group *1*, and will precede group *2*, which would result in the incorrect sequencing in the steps described further on).

As with numbering related groups of information described for a journal and cards, above, choose a method for numbering subsidiary groups of information, and use this method for your labels in your digital files.

Later, you will use this numbering system for your corresponding provisional headings and subheadings within your outline and draft digital files.

By using your file management program, you will be able to copy your labels from your preview pane and paste these into your outline file, as provisional paragraph headings and subheadings. At a later stage, you will be able to copy the content from your digital files using your preview pane. This method will save you time when constructing your outline, as well as your draft.

Types of outline

Now that you have sorted your information into groups headed by numbered labels, you are ready to create an outline for your text. You could also think of this as a map, or a plan, for your text.

As with brainstorming, in 'Stage 1 (water)', you could use a graphic way of doing your outline (graphic outline or concept map), or you could do it in list form (linear outline). Both graphic and linear outlines (not concept maps) involve hierarchical structuring and using your group labels as paragraph headings and subheadings.

Graphic outline

To produce a graphic outline, at the top – or in the top left or right corner – of a page, draw a box, circle or other shape containing the title of your text. Next, parallel to this, but at a lower level, draw shapes containing your first-level group labels – see Figure 9, below.

If you used a journal, you will find your first-level group labels in your right column or above your sentences in your first column, or in both locations, depending on the method that you used; if you used cards, you will find these on the tops of your piles; if you used digital files, you will see these in the labels displayed in the preview pane of your file management system, and in the tags or categories displayed in your file management system, if you used these. Alternatively, you could open your files to obtain them.

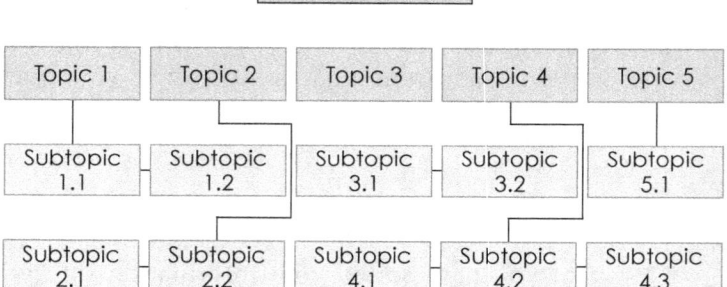

Figure 9: Group labels used as topic and subtopic headings in a graphic outline.

Now, for your second-level group labels representing your associated, but subsidiary, groups, draw lines extending vertically down from your first-level shapes to join up with your second-level shapes. In these, include all of your second-level group labels. Stagger your lines if necessary so that there is sufficient space on your page to accommodate all of your second-level labels. After each level is completed, move onto the next level, until you have connected all of the provisional headings for each topic and subtopic.

Linear outline

Head up your page with the title of your text. To produce a linear outline using your word processing application, you could start off with a bulleted list and then at a later stage convert this to a multilevel numbered list. Alternatively, you could start off with a multilevel numbered list. If you are writing up your list, you will do this manually. When you have decided on a system, enter your first-level group labels – see Figure 10, below.

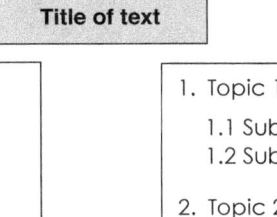

Figure 10: Group labels used as topic and subtopic headings in a linear outline, using bullets (left) and in a multilevel numbered list (right).

As with your graphic outline, if you used a journal, you will find these labels in your right column or above your sentences in your first column, or in both locations, depending on the method that you used; if you used cards, you will find these on the tops of your piles; if you used digital files, you will find these within your files, and in your preview pane, in your tags, categories and labels columns (if you added them here), displayed in your file management program.

Next, enter your second-level group labels. Do this using the bullets or numbering function available in most word processing programs; use your 'enter' or 'return' key to create a new line and your tab key to indent your list for your second-level group labels.

Continue entering all of your group labels, placing them in the correct sequence and ranking (first-level, second-level, third-level, and so on) until you have entered them all.

Concept maps – for fiction

For fiction writing, you may want to label your groups as well as the relationships between them. Concept maps are suited to this, in that the groups as well as the linking, or relationship, lines can be labelled. We could, for example, have scenes in the concept map for a fiction text linked by a line labelled 'flashback' – see Figure 11, below.

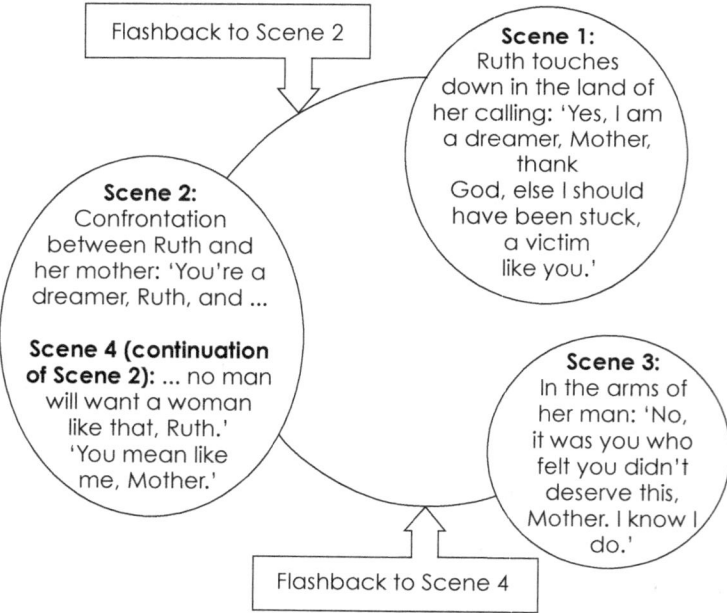

Figure 11: Paragraph labels used as scene headings in a concept map, with labelling of linking lines (relationships) between concepts (scenes); in outlines, the wording is provisional, used only to identify scenes.

Paragraphing

As you will have gathered from the previous sections, paragraphs are groups of similar, closely related information. Just as you would group items in your bedroom and kitchen cupboards and drawers according to certain criteria, with similarity being the overriding criterion, so you should group sentences in your texts into paragraphs according to a set of determining factors or criteria. One term used for this similarity is *topic*. Paragraphs usually contain a topic sentence, which encapsulates or summarizes the content of the paragraph. The remaining sentences contain various forms of supporting information. These can include explanations, causes, effects, and examples.

Types of arrangement

Some of the types of arrangement are as follows:

- Temporal (time)
- Spatial (space)
- Importance
- Cause and effect
- Comparison and contrast

Temporal

An example of arranging paragraphs temporally, or in terms of time, would be a travel article with the paragraphs ordered according to the itinerary of the traveller. The temporal pattern could be continued within the paragraphs.

Spatial

Using the same example as above, the writer could have arranged the paragraphs in terms of geography, or the places visited. This would be an example of the spatial arrangement of paragraphs. As with a temporal arrangement, a spatial arrangement could be continued within the paragraphs.

Importance

Paragraphs arranged according to importance would entail dealing with the most important aspects first, followed by the least important aspects. Alternatively, this order could be reversed. Again, this pattern of arrangement could be continued within the paragraphs.

Cause and effect

With texts arranged according to cause and effect, the causes could be listed first, followed by the effects. Alternatively, the effects could be listed first, followed by the causes. Another arrangement would entail dealing with one cause and its resultant effects, followed by another cause and its resultant effects, and so on. In this case each cause and its resultant effects would be placed in its own paragraph.

This method of arranging paragraphs could be combined with arranging the information in order of importance. This would entail dealing with the most important causes first, or the most important effects first, or vice versa, depending on how you have chosen to arrange your paragraphs.

Comparison and contrast

Following the same structure as the cause and effect method, you could arrange your information by comparing objects, items or aspects. This could entail listing all of the similarities, followed by all of the differences. Alternatively, you could choose one object or item to compare with another, or others, and deal with each related similarity and difference, followed by the next related similarity and difference, and so on.

As shown for the types of arrangement dealt with above, there are various combinations of patterns of arrangement.

The important thing is that the arrangement is coherent, unless your paragraphs are deliberately incoherent, for example, as a literary device in fiction to show the incoherence of the character, or characters, involved.

While retaining coherence and logical sequencing, the visual appeal of your paragraphs should also be taken into consideration. If your paragraphs are very long, thus presenting a visual – and, hence, psychological – barrier to reading them, consider breaking them into two or more paragraphs, while retaining your topical grouping of information. This would mean finding the logical place to divide your paragraph.

Topic sentences

Texts that explain or provide information are known as expository texts. In these texts, and in some other types of texts, each paragraph has a topic, or focus, sentence.

As the name suggests, a topic sentence summarizes the topic of the paragraph. It also offers an insight or makes a claim that contributes to the meaning of the text as a whole. Other sentences within the paragraph are used to explain, compare or support this insight or claim. The function of topic sentences in relating the paragraphs to the subject, topic, or main theme of the text is sometimes referred to as the 'golden thread' that runs through expository texts, holding them together and, in the process, promoting textual cohesion and, hence, coherence. These concepts are covered in the next chapter – 'Stage 3 (earth)'.

Doing it your way

While many people prefer to arrange their information by first using an outline, you may prefer not to do this, moving directly to writing your draft. Experiment with each method and decide which suits you best.

Summary

The appropriate state of mind for the organizing and outlining (air) stage is one that provides structure and impetus. This is considered to be a right-dominant state of mind, with limited left-state integration. An awareness of your SPAMM (subject, purpose, audience, medium, message) will encourage increased, though still secondary, L-state activity, which is the appropriate mind state (R-L state) for this stage. With this awareness, you might have had to return to the generating and research stage (water) if you had omitted any material necessary to continue.

In this chapter we looked at how to organize the information you generated, collected and researched in the water stage. This is done using the three systems proposed for storing and collecting your information, namely, a journal, or notebook, cards and digital files. Subsequently, we looked at how to arrange this information to produce an outline for your draft.

In the next chapter – the earth stage – we will look at writing and revising your draft. Here the techniques and tools are described for producing texts that effectively convey what you wish to communicate.

STAGE 3 (EARTH)

WRITING AND REVISING

Introduction

In 'Stage 3 (earth)' of the natural creative process, the stage-appropriate mind state is L-R state, which is an integrated mind state, and brain mode, with L-state/-mode dominance. While the emphasis during the early part of this stage will be on producing a draft, there will be an increasing emphasis on analysis and evaluation as you repeatedly revise your draft.

With your understanding of the creative process and how this applies to writing, you used the tools provided in 'Stage 1 (water)' to generate ideas and subsequently to research these (subject of your message).

Having organized and arranged your now researched ideas using the organizing tools described in 'Stage 2 (air)', you arrived at a provisional, or tentative, outline, or wireframe.

The next step is to write your draft text. But before you do this, there are a few preparatory steps to take, and we look at these in the next sections.

After you have produced a draft text, the next step will be to revise it, which will entail adding information, removing information, and rewriting in some places. You will also want to ensure that your text is well written, and to do this you will need to know what makes for good writing.

Having revised your text to the best of your ability, it would be useful to get some feedback on what you have written. For this reason, we look at writers' groups, toward the end of this chapter.

Revising outcomes and goals

At this point, it would be useful to revisit the envisaged outcomes of your delivered message, and the goals that you set to achieve these, if you had started to consider these prior to this point. Also, bear in mind that your objectives and goals could change as the creative process progresses. For this reason, your outcomes and goals should be reviewed at the beginning of each subsequent stage.

Revisiting SPAMM

During the previous stage, and before you organized your information and outlined your draft, you started to consider your SPAMM (subject, purpose, audience, medium, message). The reason for this was that you needed your SPAMM to become both a conscious and a background, subconscious consideration that would guide you in organizing and outlining your draft.

Prior to this – during the generating and research (water) stage – your emphasis would have been on what you wanted to say (subject), without giving too much consideration to how you would be saying it. Subsequently, though, you would need to consider more consciously why (purpose) you want to tell, who (audience) you want to tell, and how (medium) you want to tell. These factors together comprise your final text in its delivered form (message).

Revising your outcomes and goals also may result in an altered SPAMM. This might entail having to go back to a previous stage or stages. Therefore, all aspects of your text should be viewed as provisional, especially during the first three stages, or until your text is ready for delivery. This includes your SPAMM which also should be reviewed at the beginning of each subsequent stage.

Getting ready to write your draft

As you prepare to write your draft, your emphasis will shift to how you convey your content, that is how to put into words what you wish to express.

For academic writing, this will entail reporting on your research and your findings; for other types of non-fiction, you will need to impart what it is that you wish to explain or describe; and for fiction, this will entail writing the story.

Considering your SPAMM will have an impact on the language that you use. The technical term for this is *register*. In choosing a register, you will need to consider the context of your communication. For example, you would not speak to your academic supervisor the way you speak to a friend or a brother or sister. Similarly, you would not use the same language for an academic thesis as you would for an email to your closest friend. Hence, your SPAMM (your context) will determine your choice of language.

Time to write

With your chart outline, your linear outline or your concept map, and your notes in the form of your journal, cards, or digital files ready to hand, write your draft text.

At this stage of the creative process, it is important just to write down, type up, or copy and paste your content, organized according to your outline. While you will be guided by your SPAMM in the register that you use, which will dictate the words that you choose, your emphasis should be on the correct arrangement and sequencing of your content.

Hence, your emphasis at this point should not be on spelling, language structuring, and punctuation. You will consider these aspects of your text when you revise it.

Structure of the essay

While this book covers the core aspects of all forms of writing, in this section we look specifically at the structure of the essay.

Introduction

In the introduction of an essay, you present what you are going to say in the body of your text. Thus, the introductory paragraph provides a preview of the content of your essay. It also summarizes what is to be dealt with, argued or explained in the body of the essay.

Body

The paragraphs comprising the body of your essay deal with, argue or explain what you summarized in your introduction. Each topic sentence deals with an aspect of your subject, and your supporting sentences reinforce your topic sentence.

Conclusion

In the conclusion of your essay, you review what you have said in the body. Thus, the concluding paragraph sums up what was dealt with, argued or explained in the body of the essay.

Time to revise

Having written your draft text, take a break to celebrate having reached this point. The break also represents a shift into greater L-state dominance. From here on you will be focusing in greater detail on how you convey your message. This implies an increasing focus on your readers' experience. Before you start to revise your text, though, there are some considerations that you will need to bear in mind, and we look at these next.

Style

All texts are written in a particular style. Here, *style* can be used in at least two main senses. In the first sense, *style* relates to the writer's voice, the particular way that individuals express themselves in writing. While each writer's voice has an underlying character, writers will adapt their style to the occasion; in other words, according to the context – as spelt out in their SPAMM.

In the second sense, *style* relates to consistency of language usage and the visual aspects of the text. Consistency of language usage covers aspects such as spelling, hyphenation, capitalization and contractions where there is more than one way of correctly applying these. An example of a style choice in terms of spelling would be the variable spelling of *gray/grey* dependent on whether American English (AmE) or British English (BrE) has been selected as the language for your text. An example of style as it applies to the visual aspects of a text would be the font chosen (for example, Times New Roman, Verdana), the font style (for example, regular – or roman – italic, bold), and the font size (for example, 12 point, 14 point, 16 point) for the different heading levels in a text. Another aspect would be the numbering system to be used for the different heading levels, as would be the format of your in-text references and your reference section, or bibliography.

Before you start to revise your text, it would be best for you to select the styles applicable to your text. Not doing so may mean that your manuscript will be less appealing to potential publishers, as they will have to apply additional resources to styling and editing it. If you have not styled your manuscript and you decide to have it copy-edited before you submit it to a publisher, or publish it yourself, the copy-editor will need to know which styles you wish to apply. Also, there will probably be an additional charge for the styling. Therefore, giving some thought to the styles you wish to apply to your text and, preferably, applying them before you start to revise it would be optimal in terms of process.

To do this, you could select your styles from one or more style manuals and style guides, and then record these in your own style guide or style sheet, or in both. The following sections describe style manuals, style guides and style sheets in more detail.

Style manuals

Style manuals record the preferred or recommended conventions of a broad community of users, for example, APA (the American Psychological Association). They can also be aimed more broadly than at a single community of users, covering style options or suggesting styles, for example, *New Hart's Rules*, published by Oxford University Press.

Style guides

Style guides – sometimes referred to as house style – record the preferred, recommended or stipulated conventions of a specific community of users, for example, a corporation, a university department, or a publishing house. They could also apply to just one publication or to publications in a series.

Style sheets

A style sheet relates to a document, a manuscript or a publication. It is used to record instances not dealt with in a particular style guide. It is also used to record styles where no style manual or style guide has been stipulated or provided.

Whether or not there is a style manual or a style guide, or both, applicable to the text you are writing, you will need to create a style sheet. Here, you will record style decisions taken – whether these deviate from, complement or are a substitute for a style manual or style guide – even if this is just an alphabetical listing of entries, including words or other areas, and how they are to be dealt with.

This would involve recording, for example, the chosen way of spelling a word where there are spelling variations for it, as well as compounding (or hyphenation) decisions taken, among others.

In the 'Introduction', one of the reasons given for writing was to externalize your ideas so that you could gain clarity on these. You also do it to communicate your ideas and decisions with other team members while bringing your projects into being. The process involved in writing your text and having it published is no different, and also requires the externalization of your ideas and requirements in writing. Therefore, the purpose of a style sheet is to record and communicate style decisions taken.

The document that records these style decisions, the style sheet, is usually distributed to all parties working on publishing the manuscript, for example, in a publishing house. Because of repeated use and distribution of the style sheet, it has to be dated, and it has to be distributed regularly to all parties involved or, at least, whenever a new party joins the team or there is a switch in roles or functions.

The reader reigns

When you revise your text, your readers' experience should be your primary consideration. Your readers should not have to work unduly hard to derive your intended meaning. Good writing is aimed at making your readers' task as light and as easy-going as possible. Beyond this, it is aimed at engaging your readers and keeping them engaged, as well as making reading your text a pleasure. This will result in a good reading experience for your readers, which will reflect positively on you, the writer.

The more clearly, economically and vibrantly you have expressed yourself in the way you have written, the more pleasant your readers' experience will be.

In order to understand the importance of this, it is necessary to look at the psychological concept of *closure*. When a stimulus is incomplete, the human brain tends to fill in the gaps to arrive at both a complete form and a clear meaning. There are two types of closure in writing.

The first type of closure is intentional and desirable, and an example of this in writing is ellipsis. Here the reader has to reconstruct the missing parts, but the cues given enable the reader to do so with ease. In both writing and visual art, closure can be used as a device to allow the reader or viewer to participate in constructing meaning. An example of this in visual art is impressionism. In turn, participation implies engagement.

The second type of closure is unintentional and undesirable, and examples of this are errors, such as, wordy, convoluted sentences; deviations from language structuring conventions without stylistic justification; spelling errors; punctuation errors; and the like, resulting in misreadings. Your readers will reconstruct your intended meaning, but at the expense of their energy. Each time your readers have to do this, there will be an increase in frustration, often subconsciously, and this will be reflected back on you, again, often subconsciously. Therefore, do not expect your readers to reconstruct your erroneously unclear messages on your behalf. Rather invest the time and energy to prevent this, and you will reap the rewards.

Where a writer hands over the draft (otherwise known as the *first draft*), claiming that their job ends at this point, someone else will have to do both the revisions (otherwise known as the *rewriting*) and the editing, since only a small part – that of writing – of the third (earth) stage of the creative process will have been completed. This will entail considerable communication between the writer and the reviser (or rewriter), in order to bridge the gap between the writer's intended meanings and how these are reflected in the revised text. Naturally, this will come at a financial cost, and may well result in writing that does not reflect the writer's intended meanings or voice.

Furthermore, in order to ensure that the text is viewed with objective eyes, it may be worthwhile having a professional copy-editor give the text an additional edit. The parties involved in producing the text in this scenario would be the writer, the reviser – who would also do the initial edit of the text, since this is the final step in 'Stage 3 (earth)' of the natural creative process as it applies to writing – and the copy-editor.

Tight writing

Economy and diction

Every word that you use should be the best word for its role in your text. To be in the best position possible to make this decision, you must first become clear on exactly what you intend to convey. Becoming clear on this, in turn, entails being specific. This can be achieved by writing down the aspects or details that comprise what you want to convey. Another way to arrive at the right word for the job is to list all of the words that are possibilities. Use your dictionary to ensure that you understand what these words mean, and use your thesaurus to help you to find other possibilities, or synonyms. Hunt for the right, or most suitable, word until you find it.

In choosing your words, consider your SPAMM. Guided by it, use words that you envisage will be familiar to your audience. Choose the shortest and easiest route possible – by the words you choose – between your intended meaning and the minds of your readers. This means that where one word will do the work of two or more, choose that word. It may also involve a definite, real description, rather than an abstract, conceptual or philosophical one. Taking this approach may mean that a metaphor or an example could be the best way to convey your intended meaning. Also, while bearing in mind the need for variety in your writing – described further on – aim for shorter words, rather than longer ones, and aim for shorter sentences, rather than longer ones.

Providing sufficient grounds

Building your story, your claim or your description – depending on what you are writing about – involves providing the conceptual or historical basis, or background, for what you say next. To clarify this, think of a stepladder, with each step being necessary to get to the next one. Ask yourself whether there are sufficient conceptual grounds for introducing the next piece of information. Will your average reader be able to understand what you are trying to convey with the background information that you have already provided?

The concept of *closure*, introduced previously, applies here too. In the case of fiction and quasi-fiction, where the reader may have to reconstruct missing information, ask yourself whether there are sufficient cues given to enable the reader to do so, or at least to keep the reader engaged until further cues are given.

In some works of fiction and quasi-fiction, readers are left to reconstruct missing information themselves without cues. This is a literary device used to engage readers in co-creating stories or aspects of them.

Sound reasoning

Your statements must be justifiable by reasoning that is sound, effective and appropriate. Otherwise put, you must be able to support your propositions, or conclusions, with thorough and logical reasons, or premises.

The various ways to do this are not covered here, but information on this is freely available on the Internet, in libraries, and from other sources.

Relating ideas

The web of connections that relate the parts of texts to one another, holding them together and providing a sense of unity and purpose, are described by the terms *text cohesion* and *text coherence*, which are explained below.

Text cohesion

Reference is one of the devices used to link elements in a text. Referring back in a text to someone or something is known as *anaphoric* reference. In these cases, a pronoun is used instead of repeating a noun in a subsequent sentence, for example, the pronoun *He* substituting for *Mr Mandela* in the following sentences: *Mr Mandela became the first democratically elected president of the Republic of South Africa. He took his oath at the Union Buildings in Pretoria on 10 May 1994.*

Another example would be the following dialogue:

'How did you enjoy your swim?'
'I loved it!'

Referring forwards in a text to someone or something is known as *cataphoric* reference. An example of this would be the following sentences: *'The guest on our show tonight is someone who is no stranger to you: she is our public protector. Ladies and gentlemen, I present to you Thuli Madonsela.'*

Another cohesive device is ellipsis. You use this device when you omit words that are understood from the context, and therefore can be reconstructed by the reader. One example would be the following dialogue:

'When are you leaving?'
'Tomorrow.'

Instead of repeating the words *'... I will be leaving ...'*, they are omitted because they are understood, filled in, or closed, by the reader (see more on this in 'Addendum 1: Language structuring' and 'Addendum 2: Punctuation').

Conjunctions, such as *and*, *yet* and *although*, and transitional adverbs such as *next* and *then* are also used to create cohesion in texts. They do this by relating one text element to another.

Text coherence

When the meaning of a text and its parts is clear, it is coherent. The aspects of tight writing described above – ease of closure, economy, appropriate diction, sufficient grounds, and sound reasoning – all promote text coherence. Another aspect of text coherence is the clear relationships of the text elements with one another, allowing the reader to follow the unfolding meaning with ease.

Vibrant writing

If you have applied the principles set out in the previous section, your writing will already be vibrant. There are additional steps, though, that you can apply to make your writing even more vibrant.

Variety

Aiming for shorter sentences will help you to achieve economy, but this should not be at the expense of variety. It is variety in your writing that will keep your readers alert and engaged. A succession of short sentences can be just as monotonous as a series of long ones, and this lack of stimulation will make your readers work harder to stay engaged.

Varying the length, type and structure of your sentences will vary the rhythm and complexity of your text. A series of short simple sentences create a tense staccato rhythm or an indication of simplicity, depending on the context. On the other hand, longer complex, compound and compound-complex sentences (see the 'Glossary' for definitions of the sentence types) create a sense of leisure and relaxation, or an indication of complexity, again, depending on the context.

Switching rhythm will give your readers a mental break, and this will invigorate them, enabling them to stay engaged and to continue enjoying their reading experience.

Sentence length

One of the ways you can achieve variety in your writing is by varying the length of your sentences. Arranging your sentences into groups according to sentence length is yet another way to achieve variety. As mentioned previously, a series of short simple sentences can indicate a tense, nervous situation. One or more longer compound or complex sentences following these can indicate the resolution of a tense situation, with an ensuing sense of relief.

The effects produced by varying the length of your sentences will differ according to your SPAMM, one aspect of which will be whether the effects are being applied to fiction or non-fiction.

In addition to varying the length of your sentences, try to vary the length of your paragraphs. This will make your texts more visually inviting, signalling to your prospective readers that your text will offer them variety and, therefore, allow changes in rhythm and pace.

Sentence type

Switching among different types and groups of types of sentence is another way to achieve variety in your writing. Progressing from simple sentences to compound sentences to complex sentences and then to compound-complex sentences could indicate increasing complexity, and the opposite could indicate a gearing down to less complex subject matter. The effect that this will have will depend on your context, as summarized in your SPAMM. As with sentence length, the effects produced by varying the type of your sentences will differ for fiction and non-fiction.

Sentence structuring

Varying sentence structures is another way to achieve variety, which will contribute to a vibrant text.

While predominantly using the active voice – or using it where the context lends itself to the active voice – will contribute to a sense of vibrancy in your writing, the passive voice also has its uses. These include where the intention is to conceal the agent – or doer – of the action, or where the identity of the agent has not been determined or cannot be disclosed, for example, in the following sentence in a newspaper report: *'The occupants of the vehicle were all injured.'*

Also, where not naming the agent by using the passive voice will result in a construction that is more clear and concise than its active alternative, use the passive voice. This may occur where the agent does not need to be emphasized, or is insignificant, or where the agent is clear.

Other ways to vary the structure of your sentences include conjoining clauses, and adding phrases and clauses to independent clauses in one of three positions – initiating, intervening and concluding. Refer to 'Addendum 2: Punctuation' for information on how to do this.

Avoid certain nominalizations and noun chains

Nominalizations

A nominalization is the result of converting a verb or an adjective to a noun. Where this takes a derived form (for example, the *-ion* affix; also see the 'Glossary'), it makes for lacklustre writing. Using a verb or a verbal (gerund, infinitive or participle), on the other hand, makes for vibrant writing. So instead of using, for example, *the conversion of*, you could use *converting*. Here you have used one word – a verbal – instead of a derived nominalization. The *the ... of* construction is often used in academic writing, and if we convert to verbs or verbals the nominalizations among these that are not useful, the result will be far more vibrant writing, which will be more likely to keep our readers engaged.

Noun chains

When we use more than one noun to modify another noun, we have created a noun chain. An example of a noun chain is *property development planning departure proposal*, which could be converted to the *proposal for planning departures that applies to property developments*. After breaking up the noun chain and reconstructing it using words that are not nouns, the structure is longer, as in the example, but it is easier to read. While noun chains are usually the result of an attempt at precision, often they have the opposite effect, in that the reader has to invest energy unnecessarily to decipher the writer's intended meaning. This act of deciphering, or reconstructing, is an example of the undesirable closure outlined above.

Use verbs and verbals

Replacing derived forms of nominalizations with verbs or verbals results in more economical, vibrant writing. Verbs bring vibrancy to your writing, and the more demonstrative your verbs are, the less they will need to be modified by adverbs. Instead of writing *He briskly walked out of the room*, you could write *He stormed out of the room*, making the verb more demonstrative and, hence, more vigorous. The result – vibrant writing.

Tools

Reference works are the tools of every good writer. These include the following:

- Dictionary
- Thesaurus
- Encyclopaedia
- Language/grammar usage dictionary
- Language/grammar usage guide
- Discipline-specific dictionaries
- Discipline-specific guides

Here, only the first three of these reference works are discussed, as they are considered the most important.

Dictionary

Only a proper understanding of the meanings of words and possible substitutes, or synonyms, will enable us to choose the right word to convey a particular meaning in a text. Choosing the word that is most suited to its task is the basis of texts that convey economically, clearly and vibrantly what they mean. Try to use the unabridged version of one of the most recently published reputable dictionaries to do this. If you cannot obtain the unabridged version, use the concise version.

All of the print versions of the reputable dictionaries have a guide to using them, usually at the beginning. They also have lists of abbreviations used in the dictionary, usually at their beginning or end. Your dictionary should be your companion in all of your writings, and therefore, familiarizing yourself with its usage guide and abbreviations will allow you to gain maximum benefit from it.

There are also online versions of the reputable dictionaries, and you could use these too. Do check, though, that the online versions offer all of the features that the print versions offer, for example, italicization of foreign words.

Thesaurus

Do also use a thesaurus to find synonyms that could be more suitable to convey a particular meaning. Before you do so, though, ensure that you understand the meaning of the word for which you want to find a synonym. Preferably, use your dictionary to do this. Only when you have investigated the other possibilities – and understood their meanings – will you be in a position to choose the right word for the task.

When choosing and using a thesaurus, the same principles as for a dictionary apply.

Encyclopaedia

The best place to start when you are searching for information is your dictionary. When you have clarified the meanings of the words to be used in your search, you will be in a better position to build on this knowledge.

In your initial searches, focus on expanding your knowledge in your subject area, not on whether it would be permissible to quote the online encyclopaedia concerned. Use a free online encyclopaedia as a starting point: often this is where you will find the references that will be desirable and permissible to quote. This could result in an expanded Internet search or a trip to your library to borrow and read the relevant source concerned.

Getting feedback

Having revised your text one or more times, you will be in a position to get feedback. There are a number of ways you could do this. Bear in mind, though, that asking for feedback from more than one person will give you a more balanced perspective on your text.

The people who you ask for feedback could range from non-expert to expert, and you should also bear this in mind when considering the feedback given.

Writers' groups are one way of getting feedback on your text and your writing. These are structured in different ways, with some being modelled on therapeutic and support groups. Whatever the basis of their structuring, they should be a safe place to share your text while it is still in an unfinished state.

Using the feedback that you get, you could make any changes that seem to you to be necessary. Your text will remain unfinished, though, until you have edited it. After this, you may decide to have your text copy-edited by a professional copy-editor. This, in turn, may necessitate further changes.

Conventions – compliance and deviation

Readers expect compliance with the implicit conventions that determine how we structure our texts. These conventions have been studied by linguists and other scholars of language and have been recorded in various reference works. The structural conventions relating to a language are otherwise known as the grammar of a language, and the reference works that deal with them are known as language or grammar usage reference works.

Where we do not comply with the conventions governing the structuring of our texts, our readers expect an educated stylistic justification for the deviation.

Highly regarded writers such as Virginia Woolf, James Joyce, George Orwell and Doris Lessing were all experts in grammar. Notwithstanding their knowledge of language structuring, or grammar, and that these well-known writers edited their own work, their work was again edited by their publishers. This indicates the importance that good writers place on the language that they use and how they structure their texts, which results in a high standard of work produced. It also demonstrates the respect that they show for their readers.

In light of this, any notion that a thorough knowledge of language structuring will dampen or destroy one's creativity is counterintuitive. In copy-editing reference works, it is often the opinions of fiction writers (who often also wrote non-fiction) that are quoted.

Following the example set by these writers involves having a knowledge of the conventions for sequencing and connecting your text elements (words, phrases and clauses) – otherwise known as syntax and punctuation. Interestingly, some other disciplines, such as mathematics and computer programming, also have structuring (or syntactical) conventions, covering how their statements are combined.

The conventions for syntax, or how sentence components are combined, are one aspect of language structuring. Another aspect is how punctuation marks are used as an aid to combining sentence elements. For example, in certain scenarios, words can be used on their own to join text groups, while in others, a combination of words and punctuation marks can be used to join two or more text groups (phrases and clauses), and sometimes, punctuation marks alone can be used.

Because of the importance of being familiar with the conventions relating to structuring in the English language, it would be advisable for you to familiarize yourself with these. 'Addendum 1: Language structuring' and 'Addendum 2: Punctuation' set out the conventions. The 'Glossary' defines the core terms necessary to understand these Addenda.

Summary

The appropriate emphasis during the writing and revising (earth) stage is on getting the job done, or on producing a text. This is an L-state dominant stage, with limited R-state integration. During the initial part of this stage, your emphasis will be on producing your draft text, or manuscript. At this point your SPAMM (subject, purpose, audience, medium, message) is a background consideration.

However, with each revision you make, greater L-state/-mode activity will be involved. After producing your draft text, which necessitates an emphasis on generation, or production, at the expense of detail, you will arrive at the point where you will increasingly focus on detail and the context in which your text will be used. Thus, while you would need to revisit your communication outcomes and goals, as well as your SPAMM, before you write your draft, as you begin to revise your text, these will move into the foreground of your attention.

In this chapter we dealt with the structure of the essay, as a specific form of writing. We also dealt with style and how important it is to make your readers' experience as easy-going as possible. Subsequently, ways of achieving this were dealt with, and these are covered under Tight writing and Vibrant writing. Following this, we look at the tools that you will need as a writer.

After revising your text, it would be useful to get feedback on your writing, and in this chapter, we also looked at how to do this. Finally, we looked at the importance of language conventions in writing – covered in detail in Addenda 1 and 2 – because understanding these will allow us to write tight and vibrant texts.

In the next stage (fire), we will deal with editing your draft. This, too, will involve familiarity with language conventions.

STAGE 4 (FIRE)

EDITING

Introduction

To recap, in the first (water) stage, you were concerned with generating; in the second (air), with structuring; in the third (earth), with constructing. Now, in this fourth (fire) stage, your emphasis is on finishing, and this implies working with detail.

In 'Stage 1 (water)', you generated ideas and subsequently researched these. Next, in 'Stage 2 (air)', you grouped and arranged the notes you had made. Then you produced an outline, using the provisional headings you had given to your groups. In 'Stage 3 (earth)', you wrote, typed up, or copied and pasted your draft text using your outline (or wireframe) and your now organized and arranged notes. Subsequently, you revised your draft, considering your SPAMM and focusing on how best to get your message across to your readers. You did this by using tight and vibrant writing techniques and by using tools such as your dictionary, thesaurus and encyclopaedia, among other reference works.

If after revising your text to the best of your ability, you got feedback, say from fellow writers in a writers' group, you would have revised your text again to incorporate the input you received. You would now be ready to edit your revised text.

In Stage 4 (fire) of the natural creative process, the stage-appropriate mind state is L state. The emphasis during this stage will be on finishing your text and preparing it to be read by others, which could involve having your text published, or publishing it yourself.

During this stage, the emphasis on analysis and evaluation increases further. There is also a shift from subjectivity to objectivity as you distance yourself from your text and, instead, attempt to put yourself in the shoes of your prospective readers. Whereas in the previous (earth) stage, your emphasis was on conveying your content, during this (fire) stage, your emphasis is on the details, including checking for accuracy, formatting, styling, language structuring and punctuation, with the aim of preventing misreadings and ensuring the best possible reading experience for your readers.

This chapter explains what the editing stage involves.

Workflow

Before you move straight into editing your text, give some consideration to how you intend to do it, as this will optimize both time and effort. This will require a knowledge of the steps involved, which are covered below.

The concept *workflow* had its beginnings in the arrangement of assembly lines, with the goal of increased efficiency in manufacturing. Editing is similar to an assembly line, in some respects, in that it is best to break the various aspects down into rounds, or read-throughs, known among copy-editors as *passes*.

In keeping with the concept of externalizing, it would be beneficial to note down your editing strategy. As you proceed you may find that you develop and refine it further.

Working with your text, including during the editing stage, can be done at a number of hierarchical levels, as follows:

- Text
- Paragraph
- Sentence
- Word

Breaking your text down into levels is helpful when evaluating it, because it allows you to work with one aspect of it at a time, in keeping with the concept of workflow. Editing can also be broken down into the following levels, which are explained next:

- Macroediting
- Microediting

Macroediting

Editing at the level of the text – known as *macroediting* – covers aspects such as the title of the text, the headings and their numbering system, as well as captions. Stripped of the content within each section, the *macroelements* of the text remain. These are also the outline of the text.

The aspects checked during a macroedit include the fonts chosen (for example, Times New Roman, Verdana), font size (for example, 12 point, 14 point or 16 point), and the font style (for example, regular – or roman – italic and bold). These are the predominantly visual aspects of style, described in 'Stage 3 (earth): Writing and revising'.

During a macroedit, you will also check for language usage in the macroelements, including aspects such as spelling, hyphenation and capitalization, ensuring that the styles you have selected have been applied consistently.

There are two styles of capitalization that you could apply to your headings. These are *sentence-case capitalization* and *title-case capitalization.* In the case of sentence-case capitalization, only the initial letter of the title is capitalized; in the case of title-case capitalization, the main word classes (nouns, verbs, pronouns, adverbs and adjectives) are capitalized, with the other word classes (articles, prepositions and conjunctions) left uncapitalized. Note, these two styles of capitalization can vary among style manuals and style guides, so check these first.

Microediting

The aspects checked during a microedit include the level of the paragraph down to the level of the word. This refers to the content of the text, whether this is only words, or a combination of words, images and tables.

Microediting includes checking content for accuracy and coverage, but does not focus on it, because this should have been dealt with in the writing and revising (earth) stage. The elements that must be checked during a microedit include formatting, style (consistency of the styles applied), language structuring and punctuation. The aim of checking the last two of these is to prevent misreadings and to ensure the best possible reading experience for your readers.

Sample editing strategy

The following is one possible strategy for editing your text:

Setup: If you have not yet created a style sheet for your text, do so now.

Document preview: View your text in double page view. Skim through it, recording in your style sheet – if you have not already done this – the styles that apply to the macroelements of your text.

Pass 1: Edit your text from your existing framework of knowledge; that is, do not consult the print versions of your reference works. Use electronic references (online dictionary, thesaurus and encyclopaedia) only if it is essential to do so in order to continue; do have them open, though, in case you need to use them. Flag – make a comment, highlight, or indicate with one or more symbols, for example, an asterisk – anything that requires checking in a reference work, either electronic or print. Make brief entries in your style sheet where required.

In terms of workflow, doing the minimum of referencing – by using only online sources and electronic documents – means that you will not have to leave your computer to look something up. This will enable you to maintain momentum.

Take breaks during your first pass, and at the end of this pass. Doing so will increase your focus and accuracy.

Pass 2: This is your referencing pass. In other words, during this pass you will use your reference works to look up what you have flagged. Before starting this pass, take the print versions of your reference works, including your dictionary, thesaurus and encyclopaedia, down from your bookshelves. Also, open up your online reference works, if you have not already done this.

Now, systematically revisit and look up each flagged element in either your online or print reference works.

As with your first pass, take regular breaks during your second pass, as well as at the end of this pass.

Pass 3: This is your final pass. It entails reading through your text one last time to correct anything that you may have missed on previous passes. You probably will be surprised at how many changes you make during this pass. With the benefit of your objective perspective and your increased familiarity with your text, you will spot errors and required changes not picked up during previous passes.

Automated final check: The spelling and grammar checker of your word processing program can be used to pick up anything that you may have overlooked, which will prevent unnecessary embarrassment to you. A word of caution, though: these tools should *not* be used as a reference source or to guide you in your editing; any changes or suggestions they make should be implemented only with your *full understanding* of the change suggested and your *informed agreement* with this. Where this role is reversed, the opposite danger exists: embarrassment to you, the writer. Hence these tools should be seen only as an automated final check.

Revisiting SPAMM

As with the two previous stages, at the beginning of the editing (fire) stage, you will need to consider your SPAMM (subject, purpose, audience, medium, message). During this stage your SPAMM becomes a conscious consideration that will guide you in checking that the content of your text, as well as your styles, language and punctuation are all appropriate to the context of its delivery. The emphasis, therefore, during this stage is on appropriate packaging and presentation.

Revisiting your style

You will also need to revisit the following style documents, which were dealt with in the previous (earth) stage, depending on which of these apply:

- Style manual
- Style guide
- Style sheet

If you have quoted or obtained information from other sources, including books and web pages, when you wrote your draft text, you will have listed these possibly in two places, as follows:

1. For academic texts, at the point where these occur in your text – known as *short bibliographical (in-text) references.*

2. For most expository texts, at the end of your text, in the form of a list of the sources you consulted – known as a *bibliography*, or *references*, section.

The style that you will have applied to your short bibliographical (in-text) references – if these are required – and to your bibliography, or references section, will be covered in your style guide. If there is no style guide applicable to your text, or if your style guide does not deal with referencing, you would have incorporated it in your style sheet.

Revisiting the styles applicable to your text before you start editing will ensure that these are fresh in your memory as you do your editing passes.

Editing checklists

Another useful tool to aid you in editing your text is an editing checklist. 'Addendum 3: Editing checklists' is a comprehensive one; others are freely available on the Internet. By reading through your editing checklist before you start editing your text, you will ensure the editing criteria that you will be using are fresh in your memory as you do your editing passes. Also reading through your editing checklist after you edit your text will act as one of the final steps in ensuring that you deal with all aspects when you edit your text.

Reference works at the ready

As mentioned previously, it is advisable to have your electronic reference works open on your computer during your first pass. During your second pass, it is also advisable to have your print reference works ready to hand on your desk.

Two further reference sources are available in this book; these are 'Addendum 1: Language structuring' and 'Addendum 2: Punctuation'. If you have the e-book version of *The Natural Creative Process in Writing: A Core Writing and Editing Handbook for Everyone*, have this open on your computer during your first editing pass; if you have the print version of this book, have it ready to hand on your desk during your second editing pass.

Time to edit your revised draft

With your understanding of workflow as it applies to editing, having decided on an editing strategy, and having done the necessary preparation, you are ready to start editing your revised draft.

Work systematically through your text, making changes where necessary. Take regular breaks, as this will ensure greater accuracy, while also reducing potential occupational hazards, such as damage to your eyes and work-related musculoskeletal disorders (WMSDs), for example, carpal tunnel syndrome.

Appointing a copy-editor

When you have finished editing your text, it would be useful to appoint a copy-editor, a person who deals with accuracy, formatting, language and style in texts.

The terms *editor* and *editing* have been applied to you, the writer, because your role includes editing your draft. While you were editing, you may – even at this late stage – still have decided that substantial changes were required to your content, or to the way it was arranged.

The terms *copy-editor* and *copy-editing* are used when referring to an external edit. The reason for this is that while your copy-editor will query facts that appear to require verification, their emphasis will be on formatting, style, language structure and punctuation.

It would be useful to use a checklist when briefing your copy-editor. Your briefing checklist could contain the following elements.

Copy-editing checklist

- Timeframe.
- Fee.
- Scope of the work – specify what must be dealt with.
- Method of marking up the text, for example, on hard-copy pages or electronically, by tracking changes or by using highlights and square or curly brackets.
- Applicable style guide, or in the absence of this, style manual and style sheet to be used; alternatively, the combination of these that are to be used.
- Method for dealing with author queries and comments, for example, by telephone, by email, in an author queries/comments document, in comments in the document, or a combination of these methods.
- Time intervals for dealing with author queries and comments, for example, during the copy-editing process or at the end of the copy-editing process, after having received the copy-edited text.
- The copy-editor's availability to address queries when you are implementing the changes proposed.

Summary

The editing (fire) stage is dominated by L-state thinking. The appropriate emphasis during this stage is on the packaging and presentation of your content. Because of this, your SPAMM (subject, purpose, audience, medium, message) will be at the forefront of your mind.

During this stage you will focus on detail and the context in which your text will be used. You will assess your writing, the styles you have applied to your text, the structure of your language, and your choices of punctuation marks. These must be done by taking a critical and objective view of your text.

With your understanding of the processes involved in editing, as well as the supporting documents and tools available to you, you are in a position to edit your own text.

Finally, your text would benefit from copy-editing, preferably by a professional copy-editor, and your understanding of the process involved in contracting a copy-editor will help you to engage one.

After you have selectively implemented the changes suggested by your copy-editor, the writing of your text will be over. However, your work as a writer will continue until your text is in the hands of, and being read by your targeted readers.

Getting your text into the hands of your readers may entail publishing it locally, for example, on a university's intranet, or it may involve having it published through a publisher or publishing it independently, that is, by yourself. The various ways to do this are not covered here, but information on this is freely available on the Internet, in libraries, and from publishing services companies.

POSSIBLE PATHS

The way forward

This handbook provides a method and tools for all of the core areas of your writing projects. It will benefit those who currently write and edit, as well as those who wish to become writers and editors.

With this foundation and platform, you will be well positioned to extend your knowledge, and to pursue a career as a writer or editor.

In this book the self-management method and tools have been applied to writing; however, these can be adapted and applied to all of the natural creative processes that comprise the many different areas of your life. In doing so, you will find that your life becomes more harmonious and productive.

May your writings and your life be enriched by this publication!

ADDENDUM 1: LANGUAGE STRUCTURING

This addendum supplements 'Stage 3 (earth): Writing and revising'.

1. Language structuring basics

This section deals with the basics of language structuring, as it is necessary that you understand these before you move on to learning about the language structuring conventions described in section 2, below. In reading the following, refer to the 'Glossary' when terms are not familiar.

1.1 Parts that make up the whole

As dealt with in part in 'Stage 4 (fire)', the hierarchical order of texts is as follows, starting with the lowest level and moving up to the highest level:

- Word
- Phrase
- Clause
- Sentence
- Paragraph
- Text

Words and phrases belong to different classes (also known as lexical categories, lexical classes, and parts of speech), referred to in this book as *word* and *phrase classes*. The classes of words and phrases are divided into form classes, which tell us about the forms that they take, and function classes, which tell us about the functions that they perform in larger, containing structures.

The language structuring basics pertaining to the level of the word to the level of the sentence are dealt with below.

1.1.1 Word classes

The word classes are the following:

1.1.1.1 Non-variable word classes

The non-variable word classes are the following:

- adjective
- adverb
- conjunction
- noun
- preposition
- pronoun
- verb

1.1.1.2 Variable word classes

The variable word classes are the following:

- articles (considered by some authors to be adjectives)
- interjection (considered by some authors to be a form of adverb)

1.1.2 Phrase classes

Phrases, like words, belong to different classes, as follows:

- adjective phrase
- adverb phrase
- genitive phrase
- noun phrase
- prepositional phrase
- verb phrase

1.1.3 Clauses

It is also necessary to know the different functional elements and functional classes of these within clauses, as well as their various patterns of placement.

1.1.3.1 Functional elements within clauses

The functional elements, or classes, are as follows:

- Subject (*S*)
- Predicator (*P*)
- Object (*O*)
  – Direct object (*Od*)
  – Indirect object (*Oi*)
- Complement (*C*)
- Adverbial complement (*Ac*)
- Adverbial (*A*)

1.1.3.2 Functional clause patterns

The patterns of placement of the above functional elements within the clause are as follows (note in the column on the right, the type of verb possible for each pattern):

- *SP* [He walks.]   Intransitive verb
- *SPOd* [He caught it.]   Transitive verb
- *SPOi* [She served him.]   Transitive verb
- *SPOiOd* [She sold him the book.]   Transitive verb
- *SPC* [He is kind/a nurse.]   Intransitive verb: linking, or copular
- *SPOdC* [He proved her wrong/a liar.]   Transitive verb
- *SPAc* [He is there.]/[She thinks about it.]   Intransitive verb: linking, or copular
- *SPOdAc* [He put it there.]   Transitive verb
- *SPOA* [I like her very much.]   Transitive verb

From the above, you will notice that certain word classes are used as the different functional elements, or in the different clause patterns. Thus, you could also think of these functional elements as slots that can be occupied by certain classes of words and phrases. For example, noun phrases, nouns and pronouns are used as subjects, objects and complements; auxiliary and main verbs are used as predicators and adverbial phrases; adverbs and prepositional phrases are used as adverbials.

Note that adverbials are non-essential clause elements, but adverbial complements are essential clause elements. If the adverbial element can be removed without making the sentence ungrammatical, it is an adverbial; if not, it is an adverbial complement.

1.1.3.3 Verbs and what follows them

As you can see in the right-hand column of the list of clause patterns in the section on functional clause patterns, above, verbs that take a direct object are known as *transitive verbs;* those that do not take a direct object are known as *intransitive verbs*; those that take a complement are a type of intransitive verb known as a *linking verb,* or *copula.*

Transitive verbs transfer the action represented by the verb from the subject to the object. Intransitive verbs do not require an object, whereas linking verbs are a form of intransitive verb that require another word or phrase to complete them; thus they link the subject to the complement.

1.1.3.4 Binary analysis of clauses

The most important tool in being able to correctly analyse, or parse, sentences is a primary analysis of clauses into two parts, which we could call a binary analysis. Look at the patterns of placement of the functional elements within the clauses above, and you will notice that the presence of the first two elements – the SP, or subject and predicator – remains constant throughout.

In a binary analysis, we group the P (predicator) and everything else in the clause other than the subject under the term *predicate*. Note that while *predicator* is another name for the *verb phrase,* the *predicate* includes the predicator and everything else in the clause, other than the subject.

Always first doing a binary analysis of your clauses will simplify your task of further analysing them. After having broken your clauses down into subject and predicate, you will be in a better position to break the predicate down into its different components, for example, object – direct or indirect – complement, adverbial complement and adverbial (see the function classes of words and phrases, above). With this knowledge you will be well positioned to structure and punctuate your sentences, described in 2. Language structuring conventions, below, and 'Addendum 2: Punctuation'.

1.1.4 Sentences

1.1.4.1 Sentence types

The syntactical approach to punctuating implies a knowledge of syntax – hence language structuring – making it objective and scientific; the visual approach entails punctuating subjectively according to the punctuator's subjective visual criteria or to what visually appears to the punctuator to be a balanced distribution – not too cluttered or too sparse – of punctuation marks on a page or within a paragraph; the aural approach entails punctuating subjectively according to the duration of a pause, with pauses of certain durations equating to particular punctuation marks. Naturally, the syntactical approach is recommended, and is the one taken in this book.

This said, when there appears to be more than one way of punctuating a sentence using the syntactical approach, the visual or aural approach or both may be used to assist the writer to make a decision.

Taking a syntactical approach – rather than a visual or aural approach – to punctuation entails knowing about and being able to identify the four types of sentences.

With this knowledge, and by primarily taking a binary approach to analysing clauses, you will be able to punctuate your texts with ease and confidence.

The following definitions are taken from the 'Glossary':

Simple sentence – a sentence consisting of only one clause

Compound sentence – a sentence consisting of two or more independent clauses

Complex sentence – a sentence that has at least one dependent clause

Compound-complex sentence – a sentence that consists of at least two independent clauses, one of which is modified by a dependent clause

Compound sentences and compound predicates

Understanding the difference between compound sentences and compound predicates will enable you to punctuate both correctly.

As stated above, a compound sentence consists of two or more independent clauses; however, a clause with a compound predicate has one subject and two predicates.

Example – Compound sentence: I love you, and that is why I am taking this firm stance.

Example – Compound predicate, no comma required: Peter loves running and wakes up early to train.

Example – Compound predicate, comma required: We will deliver our speech, and address the issues raised.

Only where there is the possibility of a misreading should a comma precede the second predicate. This could happen where the second predicator is read as a unit together with a preceding clause element.

2. Language structuring conventions

2.1 Agreement

2.1.1 Pronoun agreement

- Pronouns must have only one likely antecedent.
- Pronouns must agree with their antecedents in:
  - person
  - number
  - gender
  - case

2.1.2 Verb agreement

- Verbs must agree in person with their subjects. Where the agreement in form conflicts with the intended meaning, or where there is confusion as to the more suitable form of agreement of the verb, the more applicable of the following principles apply: notion (agreement determined by the meaning of the subject, not its form) and attraction (agreement determined by the form of the nearest subject, not its compound form), with the latter applying in speech and informal writing, but not in formal writing.
- Verbs must also agree in number with their subjects. As with agreement in person, above, where the agreement in form conflicts with the intended meaning, or where there is confusion as to the more suitable form of agreement of the verb, the more applicable of the following principles apply: notion and attraction, with the latter applying in speech and informal writing, but not in formal writing.
- Nouns in the predicate do not influence subject-verb agreement.

2.2 Case

2.2.1 Case of pronouns

- Pronominal objects of prepositions must be in the objective case.
- Pronominal objects (direct or indirect) of verbs or verbals must be in the objective case in formal writing, but not in informal writing where the subjective case seems normal.
- Pronominal subjects of gerunds must be in the possessive case, other than where this is not possible.
- Pronominal subjects of verbs must be in the subjective case.
- Pronouns as subject complements must be in the subjective case in formal writing, but not necessarily in speech and informal writing.

- Pronouns in apposition must be in the correct form.
- Pronouns in compound subjects must be of the same form.
- Pronouns must be determined by the clauses in which they occur.
- Pronouns substituting omitted clauses must be in the correct form.

2.3 Modifiers

2.3.1 Choice, placement and reference of modifiers

Modifiers are a group that includes words, phrases and clauses that have an adverbial or adjectival function. The correct type, or class, of modifier must be chosen, and it must be placed so that it modifies only the word or construction that it was intended to modify. The subject that it refers to must be present, and the reference to what it modifies must be clear.

Errors in placing modifiers are referred to as misplaced modifiers; those where the subject is not present or where reference to the subject is not clear are referred to as dangling modifiers.

2.3.1.1 Choice of modifiers

The correct type of modifier must be used to modify what it is intended to modify. Errors that involve the incorrect class of word used to modify involve the following:

- Adjectives erroneously used as adverbs
- Adverbs erroneously used as adjectives
- Possessives erroneously used as nouns; this excludes the independent possessive, which is not dependent on a noun (the independent possessives are the following: his, hers, mine, its, theirs, ours, yours)

2.3.1.2 Misplaced modifiers

Errors, ambiguity and clumsy constructions can arise with the incorrect placement and punctuation of, or involving the following:

- Adjectives and series of adjectives
- Adverbs
- Dependent clauses
- Participles and participial phrases
- Prepositional phrases
- Split infinitives

2.3.1.3 Dangling modifiers

The following, among others, could be instances of dangling modifiers:

- Participles; the following are participles that do not dangle –
  - Absolute constructions
  - Sentence modifiers
- Adjectival phrases
- Adverbial phrases
- Appositional phrases
- Prepositional phrases
- Infinitives

2.4 Mood

The indicative mood is used to express how things are perceived by the writer or speaker; the imperative to give commands; the subjunctive to express possibility.

Tense as applied to the subjunctive mood takes the following forms:

- <u>Past</u>: *was* must be used for desirable or possible situations or actions, or for situations or actions that were required in certain situations or under certain conditions in the past.
- <u>Present or future</u>: *were* must be used for desirable or possible situations or actions, or for situations or actions that are required in certain situations or under certain conditions in the present or future.

2.5 Sentence structuring

2.5.1 Ellipsis

As mentioned in 'Stage 3 (earth)', ellipsis is a cohesive textual device; however, omitting words must be done only under the following conditions:

- Where words have been omitted, it must be easy and unambiguous for the reader to fill them in.
- Words that are necessary grammatically must not be omitted.
- Redundant words and phrases must be omitted, but this must not be at the expense of character, clarity, rhythm and flow.

2.5.2 Sentence fragments

A sentence fragment is a group of words that begins with a capital letter and ends with a terminal punctuation mark but that does not contain at least one independent clause, and therefore, is not independent. Sentence fragments are acceptable only for justifiable stylistic reasons, and they must be used sparingly.

Example – justifiable stylistic effect: Should I have to accept this behaviour? Absolutely not!

Example – not justifiable (an error): South Africa during the '80s was in turmoil. Because impatience was growing, and the passive resistance movement was gaining traction.

2.5.3 Parallelism

Where a pattern of parallelism among sentence elements is evident in terms of meaning and grammatical function, this must be reflected in the parallel grammatical form of the elements. An example of this is the famous quotation by the late former President of the United States of America John F. Kennedy (parallel elements italicized): 'Let every nation know, whether it wishes us well or ill, that we shall *pay any price, bear any burden, meet any hardship, support any friend, oppose any foe* to assure the survival and the success of liberty.'

2.6 Tense

The forms that the verb, verb phrase, or predicator, take are as follows (the first form is simple and the remaining forms are compound, reflecting both tense and aspect):

- Simple tense:
    - Past: regular and irregular past tense verbs must be used for actions that occur in the past.
    - Present: regular and irregular present tense verbs must be used for actions that occur in the present.
    - Future: *will* + regular and irregular present tense verbs must be used for actions that occur in the future.

- Perfect tense:
    - Past: *had* + past participle must be used for actions that occur before another in the past.
    - Present: *has/have* + past participle must be used for actions that occur before another in the present.
    - Future: *will have/shall have* + past participle must be used for actions that occur before another in the future.

- Progressive/continuous tense:
    - Past: *was/were* + present participle must be used for ongoing actions that occur in the past.
    - Present: *am/is/are* + present participle must be used for ongoing actions that occur in the present.
    - Future: *will have/shall have* + *been* + present participle must be used for ongoing actions that occur in the future.

- Perfect progressive/continuous tense:
    - Past: *had* + *been* + present participle must be used for ongoing actions that occur before another in the past.
    - Present: *has/have* + *been* + present participle must be used for ongoing actions that occur before another in the present.

- Future: *will have/shall have* + *been* + present participle must be used for ongoing actions that occur before another in the future.

- Passive simple tense:
  - Past: *was/were* + past participle must be used for the passive reporting of actions that occur in the past.
  - Present: *is/are* + past participle must be used for the passive reporting of actions that occur in the present.
  - Future: *will be/shall be* + past participle must be used for the passive reporting of actions that occur in the future.

- Passive perfect tense:
  - Past: *had been* + past participle must be used for actions that occur before another in the past.
  - Present: *has been/have been* + past participle must be used for actions that occur before another in the present.
  - Future: *will/shall* + *have been* + past participle must be used for actions that occur before another in the future.

- Passive progressive/continuous tense:
  - Past: *was/were* + *being* + past participle must be used for ongoing actions that occur in the past.
  - Present: *am/is/are* + *being* + past participle must be used for ongoing actions that occur in the present.
  - Future: **will/shall* + *be being* + past participle must be used for ongoing actions that occur in the future (*rarely used).

- Passive perfect progressive/continuous tense:
  - Past: **had* + *been being* + past participle must be used for ongoing actions that occur before another in the past (*rarely used).
  - Present: **has/have* + *been being* + past participle must be used for ongoing actions that occur before another in the present (*rarely used).
  - Future: **will have/shall have* + *been being* + past participle must be used for ongoing actions that occur before another in the future (*rarely used).

ADDENDUM 2: PUNCTUATION

This addendum supplements 'Stage 3 (earth): Writing and revising' and 'Stage 4 (fire): Editing'.

Punctuation

As you will realize when you read through the main uses of punctuation, many of our decisions regarding the choice and placement of punctuation marks revolve around identifying clauses, and particularly independent clauses. If you are not familiar with these terms, turn to the 'Glossary', where these are defined and explained.

If you have not read the entire 'Glossary', doing so now might be useful to familiarize yourself with the terms used in this Addendum.

Three main uses of punctuation

With these definitions in mind, we can examine the three main uses of punctuation, together with the punctuation marks for these. Note, just as numerous words belong to more than one class, dependent on their use, so many of the punctuation marks can be used for one or more of the three main punctuation usage types, for example, the period used to terminate a sentence and to indicate certain abbreviations.

The three main uses of punctuation are the following:
1. Indicating
2. Demarcating
3. Terminating

Next, we look at each of these in the order that they are listed above.

1. Indicating

Quotation marks are used to indicate the following:

1. Possession
2. Omission
3. Distancing, dialect and slang
4. Quotations
5. Titles of short works and parts of larger works

Font style – in the form of italic and bold – is used to indicate the following:

6. Titles of published stand-alone works
7. Names of craft and vehicles
8. Emphasis, highlighting and function
9. Foreign words and phrases

These main uses of punctuation and formatting for indicating are described below.

1.1 Indicating possession

An apostrophe followed by the letter *s* (*-'s*) indicates possession by a singular entity or plural entities whose nouns do not end in an *s*. Where the entity is plural and its noun is regular (that is, formed by adding *-s* or *-es*), the apostrophe follows the *s* (*-s'* or *-es'*). Where a noun ends in *y*, and its plural is created by replacing the *y* with *ies*, the *s* is followed by an apostrophe (*-ies'*).

Possession by most entities whose names end in an *s* take an apostrophe followed by *s* (*-'s*); however, there are two exceptions. The first of these is where the last syllable comprises more than one sibilant (a hissing sound); the second is where a classical name ends in an *s*.

Example – singular noun: My dog's bones are stronger since I have been giving him a calcium supplement.

Example – regular plural noun: Sadly, rhinos' horns and elephants' tusks are in demand.

Example – irregular plural noun: Our children's toys have all been bought with the goal of making learning fun.

Example – plural noun ending in -ies: Many countries' flags were adopted in the 19th and 20th centuries.

Example – last syllable comprises more than one sibilant: Hippasus' discovery of the existence of irrational numbers was believed to have led to his death by drowning.

Example – classical name ending in -s: Empedocles' cosmogony encompassed the notion of the world as having been created of matter and ether.

1.2 Indicating omission

The left column below sets out the different instances of omission and the right column gives the punctuation mark used to indicate this. Explanations follow these.

Omitted letters/s and word/s	Punctuation mark
Omitted letter/s within a word (contraction)	Apostrophe
Omitted letter/s within a word (substitution)	Em dash or two-em dash
Omitted letter/s at the end of words (abbreviation)	Period
Omitted word/s in parallel constructions (repetition ellipsis)	Comma or semicolon
Omitted word/s in a quotation (substitution ellipsis)	Ellipses (three successive points)

Omitted letter/s within a word – contraction

The apostrophe is used to indicate one or more omitted letters in a word. Ensure that the apostrophe is appropriate in terms of your register and that it is in the correct position, for example, *can't*. Also ensure that you have used the correct typographical mark. When in doubt consult the latest edition of a reputable dictionary.

Omitted letter/s within a word – substitution

The em dash (—) or two-em dash (——) is used to indicate the omission of a portion of a word by scholars where letters are illegible in a source text. They are also used by writers and publishers to replace portions of expletives ('F— that!' he said).

Omitted letter/s at the end of a word – abbreviation

The tendency for British English (BrE) is that if the letter ending the abbreviation is the same as the letter ending the full term, no period is required. Where it is not the same, use a period. So, the abbreviation for *Professor* is *Prof.* but the abbreviation for *Doctor* is *Dr*, with no period following the *r* because the full term ends with an *r*. In American English (AmE), the tendency is always to use a period. When in doubt consult the latest edition of a reputable dictionary.

Omitted word/s in parallel constructions – repetition ellipsis

The punctuation for indicating omitted words in parallel constructions that are understood (elliptical constructions), and thus are not repeated, predominantly takes the following two forms.

With compound sentences, where there are no demarcated introductory, subordinate or parenthetical elements (see Demarcating further on), a comma is sufficient:

Example: She lived in Los Angeles, he in Cape Town.

Where there are demarcated introductory, subordinate or parenthetical elements, a semicolon is required:

Example: In American football teams, there are 11 players in a side; in rugby teams, there are 15.

Omitted words in quotations – substitution ellipsis

Ellipsis points are used to indicate in quoted material where words that appear in the source text have been omitted. The terminating punctuation marks are usually retained either before or after the ellipsis points, subject to the requirements of your style guide. Where no style guide or style manual applies to your text, record the style that you have applied to terminating punctuation preceding or following ellipsis points.

1.3 Indicating distancing, dialect and slang

Use quotation marks to distance yourself, the writer, and the publisher from an assertion, to indicate the unusual usage of a term or that it is a misnomer, or to indicate that it is questionable.

Also use quotation marks to indicate dialect or slang that contrasts with the register of the text.

1.4 Indicating quotations

Quotation marks are also used to indicate direct speech and material taken from published texts.

In AmE, double quotation marks are used, with single quotation marks used within quotations; in BrE, single quotation marks are used, with double quotation marks used within quotations.

1.4.1 Quotations of direct speech

The most important difference between AmE and BrE, and the varieties that are based on these two, relates to the type of quotation marks (single versus double) used.

In AmE, double quotation marks are used for quotations, with single quotation marks used for quotations within quotations; in BrE the reverse applies.

Another difference between AmE and BrE is the positioning of commas relative to the closing quotation mark. In AmE, commas that form part of the punctuation of a passage – not of the quoted words – are placed within the closing quotation mark; in BrE, these are placed outside of the closing quotation mark if they do not form part of the quoted material, but inside, if they do.

In AmE, terminating punctuation marks (see 3. Terminating, below) routinely fall within the final quotation mark whether or not they form part of the quoted material; in BrE, their placement depends on whether they are part of the quoted material – if they are, they are placed within the final quotation mark; if not, they fall outside of it.

1.4.2 Quotations from published texts

To indicate up to 100 words of material quoted directly from published texts, enclose the quoted material in quotation marks. The AmE and BrE conventions for single versus double quotation marks also apply to quoting published material.

If a quotation extends over more than one paragraph, place a quotation mark at the beginning of every paragraph, and place a final quotation mark only at the end of the quotation.

For quotations of more than 100 words, indent the quotation from the surrounding text, and do not use quotation marks.

1.5 Indicating titles of short works and parts of larger works

Use quotation marks to indicate the titles of short works and parts of larger works such as the following:

• Short poems
• Short stories
• Songs

They should also be used to indicate parts of publications, such as the following:

• Articles in journals
• Chapters in books

In AmE, double quotation marks are used; in BrE, single quotation marks.

1.6 Indicating titles of published stand-alone works

Use italics to indicate the titles of published stand-alone works such as the following:

- Books
- Catalogues
- Epic poems
- Newspapers
- Periodicals
- Pamphlets
- Posters
- Plays
- Films
- TV and and radio series
- Albums, CDs and DVDs

1.7 Indicating names of craft and vehicles

Use italics to indicate the names of craft and vehicles such as the following:

- Aircraft
- Motor vehicles
- Ships
- Trains

1.8 Indicating emphasis, highlighting and function

Use italics to indicate emphasis or to highlight a text element. Bold can also be used to achieve this, and therefore, it is important to choose a style for a particular instance of usage, and to apply it consistently throughout the text.

Italics are used for particular predetermined functions within the text, which include the following:

- To discuss a word, phrase, or term
- To distinguish a particular function within a text, for example, for the names of word classes in dictionaries

107

Bold is also used for particular predetermined functions within the text, which include the following:

- Headings
- Headwords
- New terms on first appearance that are explained further on in the text, or elsewhere, such as in certain glossary entries

1.9 Indicating foreign words and phrases

Use italics to indicate foreign words and phrases that are still considered to be foreign, and not yet part of the English language. Where you are uncertain about whether a particular word should be italicized, consult the print version of a recently published reputable dictionary.

2. Demarcating

Sentences with only one main independent clause are known as simple sentences. Where independent clauses have dependent clauses added to them, these are known as complex sentences. Here, the relationship is one of subordination, because clauses of unequal grammatical status have been joined.

Words, phrases and clauses added to main independent clauses can occur in three positions relative to the main independent clause. These are the following:

1. Initiating (preceding the main independent clause)
2. Intervening (within the main independent clause)
3. Concluding (following the main independent clause)

Their grammatical function – defining (or restrictive) or non-defining (or non-restrictive/parenthetical), and dependence or independence – and their length determine whether or not they are demarcated from the independent clause and the type of demarcating punctuation mark that will be used to do this.

In addition to the three positions relative to the main clause described above, independent clauses can be conjoined (joined to one another). Where this happens, phrases and dependent clauses can again be added to the conjoined clauses in the positions outlined above.

A sentence with one main independent clause that is conjoined to another main independent clause is known as a compound sentence. In cases where either of the conjoined clauses have dependent clauses added to them, these are known as compound-complex sentences.

Throughout the section on demarcating, phrases are dealt with first, followed by clauses.

2.1 Initiating

2.1.1 Initiating phrases

The term *initiating phrases* also applies to single words. The grammatical type and length of an initiating phrase (a phrase preceding an independent clause) specify whether a comma is needed to demarcate it from the rest of the sentence. There are three categories of usage, and these are as follows:

1.   Comma is not permitted
2.   Comma is optional
3.   Comma is required

The conventions that cover these are set out below.

In the rare case of a list preceding an independent clause (see 2.1.1.4, below), a colon or single en dash (see the 'Glossary' for definition) is used to demarcate the initiating list.

2.1.1.1 Comma not permitted

Gerundial phrases

Where a gerundial phrase is used as the subject of a sentence, a demarcating comma must not be used after it. Doing so would entail demarcating a subject from its verb, which is not permissible.

Example: Supporting a programme that finds employment and accommodation for the homeless is one way that you can serve humankind.

Because gerundial phrases are not initiating phrases, but instead act as subjects, there is no initiating phrase convention applicable to them, as there are for the initiating phrase types below.

2.1.1.2 Comma optional

Short initiating adverbial phrase – no misreading possible

The convention for short initiating adverbial phrases that do not require a demarcating comma to prevent a misreading is given below. This is followed by the applicable formula and examples.

Short initiating adverbial phrase where no misreading is possible – no comma is necessary to demarcate the initiating adverbial phrase (IP) from the independent clause (IC).

Formula: IP (Short – three or fewer words – adverbial phrase) IC.

Example – time: In January we have the warmest and longest evenings.

Example – place: Behind the curtain you will see the start of a beautiful day.

Example – manner: By following procedure staff members support our brand.

Example – degree: After due consideration I agreed to the proposal.

Whether or not to demarcate short initiating adverbial phrases with an optional comma – where no misreading is possible without it – from the rest of the sentence will be determined by your target audience and the style adopted for this audience.

However, choosing to demarcate initiating phrases where the comma is optional could result in an unwanted staccato rhythm. It could also result in the clustering of punctuation marks where parenthetical constructions are used close to the short initiating adverbial phrase.

Example: On Tuesdays, we usually do our grocery shopping. On Wednesdays, we go to the movies. Of late, we go for day drives on Fridays. On weekends, we socialize. Since June, though, we have done nothing on Mondays.

2.1.1.3 Comma required

Other types of phrases

For all types of initiating phrases other than short initiating adverbial phrases where no misreading without the demarcating comma is possible, a comma is used to demarcate the initiating phrase from the clause introduced. These include short initiating adverbial phrases where a misreading is possible without the demarcating comma, longer initiating adverbial phrases, sentence adverbs, transitional adverbs, adjectival phrases, and participial phrases.

The conventions for initiating phrase types that require a comma to demarcate them from the independent clauses that follow them are given below. These are followed by the applicable formulae and examples.

1. **Short initiating adverbial phrase where a misreading without the demarcating comma is possible.**

Formula: IP (short – three or fewer words – adverbial phrase), IC.

Example: In any event, management scenarios differ.

Explanation: In the above example, the comma prevents the misreading of *event management* as a unit, in this case, a compound noun.

2. **Long initiating adverbial phrase.**

Formula: IP (long – four or more words – adverbial phrase), IC.

Example: Yesterday and the day before, the man was seen dancing and singing in the square.

3. **Sentence adverb.**

Formula: IP (sentence adverb), IC.

Example: Regrettably, the car will not be ready for delivery tomorrow.

4. **Transitional adverb.**

Formula: IP (transitional adverb), IC.

Example: Finally, I would like to thank all contributors for their efforts.

5. **Adjectival phrase.**

Formula: IP (adjectival phrase), IC.

Example: Of all people, John should have known better.

6. **Participial phrase.**

Formula: IP (participial phrase), IC.

Example: When preparing for an event, always ensure that you have the right equipment.

2.1.1.4 Phrase lists in initiating position

Mostly, phrase lists occur in the final position, but sometimes, for stylistic reasons, a writer may put a list in the initiating position; that is, it may precede the independent clause. In this case, a colon is used to demarcate the phrase list from the independent clause.

Example: An easel, different coloured paints, a few brushes and a canvas: these were what made his life complete.

2.1.2 Initiating clauses

As you will note in the 'Glossary', a dependent clause cannot stand alone as a grammatically independent sentence.

The convention for demarcating dependent clauses (also known as subordinate clauses because they are introduced by subordinating conjunctions, for example, *after, although, because, except, if, unless, when, whether, while*) in the initiating position is as follows:

2.1.2.1 Dependent/subordinate initiating clauses

Where a dependent clause (DC) precedes an independent clause (IC), a comma is placed after the dependent clause to demarcate it from the independent clause.

Formula: DC, IC.

Example: If you do your maths homework, I will take you out for supper.

2.1.2.2 Clause lists in initiating position

As stated previously, in the section on phrase lists in initiating position (2.1.1.4, above), clause lists also occur mostly in the final position, but sometimes, for stylistic reasons, a writer may put them in the initiating position; that is, a clause list may precede the independent clause. In this case, a colon is used to demarcate the clause list from the independent clause.

Example: Clean your room, do your homework and apologize to your sister: these are things I want you to do this afternoon.

2.2 Intervening

2.2.1 Intervening phrases

The term *intervening phrases* also applies to single words. These provide additional, non-essential information to the core meaning and functional elements of a sentence.

Pairs of commas, dashes or parentheses (brackets) are used to demarcate intervening phrases from the rest of the sentence. If you remove the intervening phrase and its demarcating punctuation, the core meaning and grammaticality of the sentence will remain intact. The uses of these three demarcating punctuation marks are given below.

2.2.1.1 Commas

There are three uses for a pair of commas as demarcators of intervening phrases, as follows:

1. **Intervening phrase is short.**

Example: Beauty, I believe, lies in the eyes of the beholder.

2. **Intervening phrase is de-emphasized or not emphasized.**

Example: Inflation, in terms of a report by the Ministry of Finance, has escalated by two percent.

3. **Intervening phrase is a non-defining appositive.**

Appositives restate an existing noun differently, sometimes introduced by *and* or *or,* or they define it. Non-defining appositives are demarcated with a pair of commas; defining appositives are not demarcated.

Example: I would like to acknowledge John Lexington-Smith, our benefactor, for his generous donation to this foundation.

2.2.1.2 Dashes

A pair of dashes have three uses as demarcators of intervening phrases, as follows:

1. **Intervening phrase is emphasized.**

Example: It is widely thought – questionably so – that the bottom line is all that matters.

2. **Intervening phrase is long.**

Example: Muhammad Ali – one of the greatest boxers of all time and one of those instances of exceptional talent – was a giant and a gentleman.

3. **Intervening phrase does not fit comfortably into the syntax of the main clause.**

Example: I cannot understand the modern approach to grammar – with it and creativity as mutually exclusive opposites – in many schools.

2.2.1.3 Parentheses

A pair of parentheses have eight main uses for demarcating de-emphasized intervening phrases, as follows:

1. **Unimportant point.**

Example: Mike Smith (Smithy) is the site foreman at the Jozini construction site.

2. **Exception.**

Example: All dogs (except for a few hairless breeds) are covered in hair.

3. **Short list of examples.**

Example: A small number of dog breeds (for example, Chinese Crested, Mexican Hairless, Peruvian Hairless) are not covered in hair.

4. **Acronyms and technical synonyms.**

Example – acronyms: The Domestic Animal Rescue Group (DARG) is one of the pro-life non-profit animal rescue organizations in South Africa that is doing fine work.

Example – technical synonyms: Random access memory (RAM) is where information that a computer is processing at any given moment is stored.

5.   Abbreviations.

Example*: Professor (Prof.)* is an example of a word in BrE that takes a period where abbreviated.

6.   Translations and scientific names.

Example – translations: He invited everyone he knew to the braai (barbecue) he was going to hold.

Example – scientific names: Great white sharks (*Carcharodon carcharias*) have been known to grow up to six metres in length.

7.   Cross-references.

Example: In our corporate manual, the part dealing with absenteeism (section 5) covers this extensively.

8.   Numerical equivalents.

Example: The high-altitude grassland region of South Africa, known as the highveld, varies between 1200 metres (3937 feet) and 1800 metres (5906 feet) above sea level.

2.2.1.4 Nesting of intervening phrase demarcators

Where intervening phrases themselves contain intervening phrases, this is known as the nesting of intervening phrases. Different demarcating punctuation marks are used to distinguish clearly between the levels of nesting.

If the primary intervening phrase is demarcated, say, with commas, demarcate the secondary, or nested, intervening phrase with a pair of either of the two remaining options, parentheses or dashes.

2.2.1.5 Incorrect placement of intervening phrase demarcators

The intervening phrase demarcators (commas, parentheses and dashes) must be placed so that they enclose only the intervening phrase.

You can test for the correct placement of the demarcators preceding and following an intervenor by reading a sentence as though the words enclosed between the demarcators were not there; the abridged sentence should still make sense.

2.2.2 Intervening clauses

2.2.2.1 Parenthetical clauses

An intervening parenthetical clause is demarcated from the surrounding sentence with a pair of dashes or a pair of parentheses. Where there is one intervening parenthetical clause or sentence, it does not take a terminal punctuation mark. (See 2.2.2.1.2 Parentheses, below, for where an intervening parenthetical element comprises two sentences.)

2.2.2.1.1 Dashes

As with intervening phrases, a pair of dashes are used in three cases, as follows:

1. **Intervening clause is emphasized.**

Example: It is widely thought – and I disagree with this – that the bottom line is all that matters.

2. **Intervening clause is long.**

Example: Joe Frazier, like Ali – Smokin' Joe was for most of his professional career a very close friend of Muhammad Ali – was also a giant and a gentleman.

3. **Intervening clause does not fit comfortably into the syntax of the main clause.**

Example: I do not support the modern approach to grammar – teachers superstitiously embrace the notion that grammar holds no appeal for anyone – which enforces the view that it is a necessary evil that should be indirectly apprehended through occasional limited exposure to it.

2.2.2.1.2 Parentheses

A pair of parentheses is used to demarcate de-emphasized intervening parenthetical clauses, similarly to intervening phrases, as follows:

1.   **Single parenthetical clause/sentence.**

Example: The most represented breeds at the dog show were the smaller ones (they accounted for two-thirds of entries), those less than 40 centimetres tall.

2.   **Where the parenthetical information consists of two sentences, the first sentence is terminated with a terminal punctuation mark (see 3. Terminating, further on), but the second one is not.**

Example: The master control panel (It is behind the watercolour painting. You will need to open the safe) is well hidden and secure.

2.2.2.2 Relative dependent clauses

Dependent clauses that intervene within the main independent clause and start with a relative adjective (*whose*), a relative adverb (*when, where*) or a relative pronoun (*that, who, which*) are known as relative dependent clauses. They are either defining or non-defining, and the conventions for punctuating them are set out below.

1.   **Defining relative clauses. These are not demarcated from the surrounding independent clause.**

Example: Soldiers who have not been properly debriefed after a battle are more likely to experience post-traumatic stress disorder.

Explanation: The relative *who* clause defines, or limits, those who *are more likely to experience post-traumatic stress disorder* as *Soldiers who have not been properly debriefed*, that is, it is a defining relative clause.

2. **Non-defining relative clauses. These are demarcated with a pair of commas from the surrounding independent clause.**

Example: Soldiers, who may have experienced trauma on the battlefield, could benefit from regular psychological assessments.

Explanation: The relative *who* clause refers to all *Soldiers*, not to only those *who may have experienced trauma on the battlefield*, that is, it is a non-defining relative clause.

The relative pronoun *which* is predominantly used in BrE for both defining and non-defining relative clauses. In AmE, the relative pronoun *that* is used for defining relative clauses, and *which* is used for non-defining relative clauses.

The American convention of reserving *that* for defining relative clauses is relaxed where *that* is used as a conjunction followed by a subsequent defining relative clause; in this case, some use *which* to introduce the subsequent defining relative clause. This convention is also relaxed to avoid a repetition of sounds (euphony), for example, This is the hat which Pat wore on the night of her arrest, not *hat that Pat*.

2.3 Concluding

2.3.1 Concluding phrases

2.3.1.1 Parenthetical phrases

The term *concluding phrases* also applies to single words. As with intervening parenthetical phrases, concluding parenthetical phrases provide additional, non-essential information to the core meaning and functional elements of a sentence. Where a phrase has been added at the end of a main independent clause, a comma, a dash or a pair of parentheses are used to demarcate it from the independent clause, and a terminating punctuation mark – period, question mark, exclamation mark, or in the case of ellipsis, a dash or ellipsis points – terminates it (see 3.

119

Terminating, below). Where a pair of parentheses is used, the terminating punctuation mark follows the closing parenthesis.

Example: John ran an extraordinary race, exhibiting enormous talent.

Example: Peter is a superb athlete – in a class of his own, actually.

Example: Barbecues have different names in different countries (*braai* in South Africa, *tandoor* in Pakistan and India, *Grillen* in Germany, to name a few).

2.3.1.2 Phrase lists

Where a phrase list follows an independent clause, including where the main independent clause contains a phrase like *the following*, a colon demarcates the list from the preceding independent clause.

This section deals with lists made up of words or phrases; however, lists can also be made up of independent clauses, and these are dealt with further on in the section on clause lists (2.3.2.2, below).

Example: I would like to do the following when I feel that I am approaching burnout: eat, sleep and play.

2.3.2 Concluding clauses

2.3.2.1 Concluding parenthetical clauses

As with intervening parenthetical clauses, concluding non-defining dependent clauses provide additional, non-essential information to the core meaning and functional elements of a sentence. Where a parenthetical dependent clause has been added at the end of a main independent clause, a comma, a dash or a pair of parentheses are used to demarcate it from the independent clause; a terminal punctuation mark (period, question mark, exclamation mark, or in the case of ellipsis, a dash or ellipsis points) terminates it (see 3. Terminating, below). As with concluding phrases, above, the terminating punctuation mark follows the closing parenthesis.

Example – one concluding parenthetical clause/sentence: The most represented breeds at the dog show were the smaller ones, those less than 40 centimetres tall (they accounted for two-thirds of entries).

Where the parenthetical information consists of a two sentences, the first sentence is terminated with a terminal punctuation mark (see 3. Terminating, further on), but the second one is not.

Example – two concluding parenthetical sentences: The master control panel is well hidden and secure (It is behind the watercolour painting. You will need to open the safe).

Sometimes, though, a clause or sentence is parenthetical within the context of the paragraph, not within a sentence. In these cases, the parenthetical sentence stands on its own, and the terminating punctuation mark is placed inside the final parenthesis.

Example – subsequent parenthetical sentence: Nelson Mandela's will reflected his life. (He distributed his considerable legitimate wealth prudently among those he loved, and the causes he supported.) His legacy is a blueprint of excellence, wisdom and generosity for generations to come.

2.3.2.2 Concluding dependent clauses

As you will note in the 'Glossary', a dependent clause cannot stand alone as a grammatically independent sentence. For the following conventions, you will also need to recall the definitions of defining and non-defining clauses.

The conventions for demarcating dependent clauses in the concluding position are as follows.

Where a defining dependent clause follows an independent clause, it is not demarcated from the preceding independent clause.

1. **Defining dependent clause (DDC) follows the independent clause (IC).**

Formula: IC DDC.

Example: I will take you to your favourite pizza place if you do your homework.

Explanation: The *if* clause specifies, or limits, what condition must be met for the resultant action, or end, to be effected.

Where a non-defining dependent clause follows an independent clause, a comma demarcates the non-defining dependent clause from the independent clause.

2. **Non-defining dependent clause (N-D DC) follows the independent clause (IC).**

Formula: IC, N-D DC.

Example: I like him very much, although not everyone else does.

Explanation: The concluding non-defining dependent clause, starting with *although* is demarcated from the preceding independent clause because it does not define or limit the independent clause.

Be aware that the distinction between defining and non-defining is often quite subtle, and when you return to your text during the final stage of the natural creative process – the editing (fire) stage – you will need to query each relative phrase and clause to see that you have punctuated it so that the correct meaning is conveyed to your readers, and therefore, that misreading are avoided.

2.3.2.3 Clause lists

A colon demarcates a clause list only where an independent clause precedes it and contains a phrase like *the following*.

Example: I want you to do the following: clean your room, do your homework and apologize to your sister.

2.4 Conjoining

Where we join two independent clauses (conjoining) to form a compound sentence, the independent clauses are demarcated from each other using any of the following:

1. A coordinating conjunction preceded by a comma
2. An adverb preceded by a semicolon and usually followed by a comma
3. A semicolon on its own
4. A dash on its own
5. A colon on its own
6. Commas where the conjoined clauses comprise a series of three short independent clauses with a common subject

Where two independent clauses are conjoined, the relationship is one of coordination, because clauses of equal grammatical status have been joined.

The effect that the writer wishes to achieve in conjoining the independent clauses will determine whether a punctuation mark is used, and if one is used, what the mark will be.

The conventions for conjoining independent clauses are given below. These are followed by the applicable formulae and examples.

1. **Independent clauses conjoined by a coordinating conjunction.**

The coordinating conjunctions are *and, but, for, nor, or, so,* and *yet.* Note that no comma is necessary where both clauses are short and where no misreading of the elements being joined by the conjunction is possible.

Formula: **IC, coordinating conjunction IC.**

Example: Mary kicked the ball with gay abandon, and John followed her around the field giving instructions as he did so.

2. Independent clauses conjoined with an adverb.

Independent clauses that are conjoined to preceding independent clauses by adverbs (*consequently, however, indeed, moreover, nevertheless, nonetheless, therefore, thus*) are demarcated by a semicolon, which precedes the adverb. This convention also applies to transitional terms (*again, for example, in addition, namely, next, subsequently*). A comma is usually placed after the adverb to demarcate the initiating adverb from the independent clause that follows it, but it is permissible to omit the demarcating comma after *thus* or *therefore* where the relationship described by the adverb is not emphasized.

Formula: IC; adverb, IC.

Example – adverb: I like his art; however, there are some people who do not.

Example – transitional adverb: Warming up before you exercise is always a wise thing to do; for example, before you go for a run, you should do a few stretches.

OR

(where the relationship described by the adverb is not emphasized)

Formula: IC; adverb IC.

Example: I was exhausted after finishing writing my book; thus I decided to take a break.

3. Independent clauses conjoined with a semicolon.

A semicolon is used to demarcate conjoined independent clauses where the relationship between the conjoined independent clauses is neutral; that is, the subsequent independent clause involves no abrupt change in idea or tone, and it does not expand on or illustrate the preceding clause.

Formula: IC; IC.

Example: I have a strong opinion on this matter; she feels less strongly about it.

4. Independent clauses conjoined with a dash.

A dash is used to demarcate the conjoined independent clauses where the subsequent independent clause involves an abrupt change in notion or tone.

Formula: IC – IC.

Example: It is thought that democracy is a growing phenomenon – in some regions, though, it is merely the facade of democracy that is a growing phenomenon.

5. Independent clauses conjoined with a colon.

A colon is used to demarcate conjoined independent clauses where the subsequent independent clause expands on or illustrates the preceding clause.

Formula: IC: IC.

Example: I love my dog: He truly is this man's best friend.

or

Example: I love my dog: he truly is this man's best friend.

The first example follows the capitalization tendency for AmE style, whereas the second one follows that of BrE style. Thus both forms of capitalization following the colon are correct, but the form selected will be determined by the applicable capitalization style.

6. Three short independent clauses with a common subject, conjoined with commas.

Commas can only be used to demarcate independent clauses from one another where there are (1) three (2) short independent clauses that (3) have an identical subject. Only where these three conditions have been met can independent clauses be conjoined by using commas as demarcating punctuation marks.

Formula: **S (same) P, S (same) P, S (same) P.**

Example: He came, he saw, he conquered.

Explanation: Commas demarcate the three independent clauses from one another.

With imperatives (commands), the implied person is *you*. In these sentences, the above conditions are met.

Formula: **S (same – implied) P, S (same – implied) P, S (same – implied) P.**

Example: Trust yourself, run like the wind, win honourably.

3. Terminating

Terminating punctuation marks end all sentences. The terminating punctuation marks are the following:
1. Period
2. Question mark
3. Exclamation mark
4. Dash (in limited cases)
5. Ellipsis points (in limited cases)

1. **Period – a period can terminate a statement (declarative sentence) and a command or request (imperative sentence).**

Formula: S (*statement*).

Example: I watched as the eagle landed gracefully.

Formula: S (*command*).

Example: Stop that behaviour.

Formula: S (*request*).

Example: Would you please ensure that your report is submitted on Monday before 8.30 a.m.

Note that where indirect questions and interrogative words – such as *why* – form part of a sentence, they are terminated with a period, not a question mark.

Example – indirect question: He asked if I know how many trees there are in the plantation.

Example – interrogative word: Don't question my personal boundaries by asking why.

2. **Question mark – a question mark terminates a direct question (interrogative sentence).**

Formula: S (*question*)?

Example: Where do you keep your shoes?

This also applies to short informal questions in dialogue.

Example: She spun around and asked 'How so?'

A direct question as the subject of a sentence is terminated with a question mark.

Example: Do we attempt a turnaround or do we liquidate? was the only item on the agenda.

3. **Exclamation mark – an exclamation mark terminates an exclamatory sentence, which includes interjections; it can also be used with commands involving strong emotion.**

Overuse of the exclamation mark to imply meanings that could be conveyed by appropriate words, suitably arranged and punctuated, is considered amateurish in formal documents and publications.

Formula: S (*exclamation*)!

Example: 'Yes!' she shouted when asked whether she would be supporting the candidate.

Formula: S (*command*)!

Example: Get me the wrench now!

4. **Dash – an en dash is used to terminate sentences in dialogue where the speaker has been interrupted.**

Formula: S (*statement*) –

Example: 'I was thinking about –' he said. Then there was silence.

Formula: S (*request or command*) –

Example: 'Get my will from –' Then the line went dead.

Formula: S (*question*) –

Example: 'How many men have we –' There was a click as the call was cut.

Formula: S (*exclamation*) –

Example: 'I will not tolerate –' Then he threw the phone down.

5. **Ellipsis points – these are used to terminate a sentence in dialogue where the speaker's or narrator's thoughts or words trail off.**

Formula: S (*statement, request, command, question or exclamation*) ...

Example: 'Mary, please ...' Then she was gone, and we watched fixated on what had been her image on our screen.

ADDENDUM 3: EDITING CHECKLISTS

This addendum supplements 'Stage 4 (fire): Editing'.

Composition checklist

Style

Style requirements

- Have you selected styles so as to ensure consistency within your text?
- Do your selected styles comply with the requirements of your audience and the medium you will be using to publish your text (review your SPAMM to establish this)?
- Have you recorded your selected styles, for example, on a style sheet?
- Have you applied your selected styles throughout your text?

Paragraphing

Type of arrangement

- If yours is an expository text that requires an introduction, a body and a conclusion, such as an essay, a thesis, or an academic paper, have these been included?
- Are your paragraphs arranged, or sequenced, according to a specific scheme, for example, temporal, spatial, importance, cause and effect, comparison and contrast?

Topic sentences for expository texts

- If yours is an expository text, do your paragraphs contain topic sentences?
- Do your topic sentences set out the main ideas or concepts of your paragraphs?

- Do your topic sentences offer insights or make claims that are related to the text as a whole?
- Is the information within your paragraphs used to explain, compare or support the insights, or claims, made in your topic sentences?

Tight writing

Economy and diction

- Is every word that you have used the best word for its role in your text?
- Are your words in the correct register for your readers (as described in your SPAMM)?

Providing sufficient grounds

- Non-fiction: Have you provided the conceptual or historical basis, or background, for your statements?
- Fiction: Have sufficient cues been given to enable the reader to reconstruct missing information, other than where you have given sufficient information only to build suspense and keep the reader engaged?

Sound reasoning

- Are your statements justifiable?
- Where required have you supported your propositions, or conclusions, with sound reasons, or premises?

Relating ideas

Text cohesion

- Reference: Have you linked elements in your texts by referring backwards and forwards using pronouns to substitute for nouns wherever this is possible?
- Ellipsis: Have you linked elements in your texts by omitting words that are understood from the context and can, therefore, be easily reconstructed by your readers?

- Conjunctions and transitions: Have you used conjunctions and transitions to link clauses and sentences to one another?

Text coherence

- Will the relationships among your text elements be clear to your readers?

Vibrant writing

Variety

- Have you varied the length of your sentences?
- Have you varied the types of your sentences (simple, compound, complex, compound-complex)?
- Have you grouped your sentences according to length and type for stylistic purposes, that is, to achieve a desired effect?
- Have you varied the structure of your sentences, for example, by using the passive voice where this is optimal, or by varying the types of clauses (dependent versus independent) used and their positioning in your sentences?
- Have you varied the length of your paragraphs?

Nominalizations

- Have you avoided derived nominalizations such as those ending with the *-ion* suffix, by replacing them wherever possible with verbals?

Noun chains

- Have you avoided noun chains by using alternative constructions that incorporate words that are not nouns?

Verbs and verb forms

- Have you used strong, demonstrative verbs and verbals wherever possible?

Language structuring checklist

Agreement

- **Pronoun agreement**
  - Does each pronoun have only one likely antecedent?
  - Does each pronoun agree with its antecedent in:
    - ◦ Person?
    - ◦ Number?
    - ◦ Gender?
    - ◦ Case?

- **Verb agreement**
  - Do verbs agree in person with their subjects? Where the agreement in form conflicts with the intended meaning or where there is confusion as to the more suitable form of agreement of the verb, has the more applicable of the following principles been applied: notion and attraction (in speech and informal writing)?
  - Do verbs agree in number with their subjects? Where the agreement in form conflicts with the intended meaning or where there is confusion as to the more suitable form of agreement of the verb, has the more applicable of the following principles been applied: notion and attraction (in speech and informal writing)?
  - Have any nouns in the predicate erroneously influenced subject-verb agreement?

Case

- **Case of pronouns**
  - Are pronominal objects of prepositions in the objective case?
  - Are pronominal objects (direct or indirect) of verbs or verbals in the objective case in formal writing?
  - Are pronominal subjects of gerunds in the possessive case, other than where this is not possible?
  - Are pronominal subjects of verbs in the subjective case?

- Are pronouns as subject complements in the subjective case in formal writing, but not necessarily in speech and informal writing?
- Are pronouns in apposition in the correct form?
- Are pronouns in compound subjects of the same form?
- Are pronouns determined by the clauses in which they occur?
- Are pronouns substituting for omitted clauses in the correct form?

Modifiers

- **Choice of modifiers**
  - Are adjectives used where adjectives are required?
  - Are adverbs used where adverbs are required?
  - Have possessives (excluding independent possessives) been used as modifiers, not as nouns?

- **Placement of modifiers**
  Have the following words and constructions been positioned and punctuated correctly?
  - Adjectives and series of adjectives
  - Adverbs
  - Dependent clauses
  - Participles and participial phrases
  - Prepositional phrases
  - Infinitives

- **Dangling modifiers**
  Do any of the following types of modifier, among others, dangle without anything to modify?
  - Participles, except the following:
    ◦ Absolute constructions
    ◦ Sentence modifiers
  - Adjectival phrases
  - Adverbial phrases
  - Appositional phrases
  - Prepositional phrases
  - Infinitives

Mood

Are tenses as they apply to the subjunctive mood used in the following ways?

- <u>Past</u>: *was* is used for desirable or possible situations or actions, or for situations or actions that were required in certain situations or under certain conditions in the past.
- <u>Present or future</u>: *were* is used for desirable or possible situations or actions, or for situations or actions that are required in certain situations or under certain conditions in the present or future.

Sentence structuring

- **Ellipsis**
  - Where words have been omitted, will it be easy and unambiguous for the reader to fill them in?
  - Have any grammatically necessary words been erroneously omitted?
  - Where redundant words and phrases have been omitted, has this erroneously been done at the expense of character, clarity, rhythm and flow?

- **Sentence fragments**
  - Have sentence fragments been used only for justifiable stylistic reasons?
  - Have sentence fragments been used sparingly?

- **Parallelism**
  - Where a pattern of parallelism among sentence elements is evident in terms of meaning and grammatical function, has this been reflected in the parallel grammatical form of the elements?

Tense

Are tenses of verbs and verb phrases, or predicators, used in the following ways?

- **Simple tense:**
  - <u>Past</u>: regular and irregular past tense verbs are used for actions that occur in the past.
  - <u>Present</u>: regular and irregular present tense verbs are used for actions that occur in the present.
  - <u>Future</u>: *will* + regular and irregular present tense verbs are used for actions that occur in the future.

- **Perfect tense:**
  - <u>Past</u>: *had* + past participle are used for actions that occur before another in the past.
  - <u>Present</u>: *has/have* + past participle are used for actions that occur before another in the present.
  - <u>Future</u>: *will have/shall have* + past participle are used for actions that occur before another in the future.

- **Progressive/continuous tense:**
  - <u>Past</u>: *was/were* + present participle are used for ongoing actions that occur in the past.
  - <u>Present</u>: *am/is/are* + present participle are used for ongoing actions that occur in the present.
  - <u>Future</u>: *will have/shall have* + *been* + past participle are used for ongoing actions that occur in the future.

- **Perfect progressive/continuous tense:**
  - <u>Past</u>: *had* + *been* + present participle are used for ongoing actions that occur before another in the past.
  - <u>Present</u>: *has/have* + *been* + present participle are used for ongoing actions that occur before another in the present.
  - <u>Future</u>: *will have/shall have* + *been* + past participle are used for ongoing actions that occur before another in the future.

- **Passive simple tense:**
  - <u>Past</u>: *was/were* + verbs + past participle are used for the passive reporting of actions that occur in the past.
  - <u>Present</u>: *is/are* + past participle are used for the passive reporting of actions that occur in the present.
  - <u>Future</u>: *will be/shall be* + past participle are used for the passive reporting of actions that occur in the future.

- **Passive perfect tense:**
  - Past: *had been* + past participle are used for actions that occur before another in the past.
  - Present: *has been/have been* + present participle are used for actions that occur before another in the present.
  - Future: *will/shall* + *have been* + past participle are used for actions that occur before another in the future.

- **Passive progressive/continuous tense:**
  - Past: *was/were* + *being* + past participle are used for ongoing actions that occur in the past.
  - Present: *am/is/are* + *being* + past participle are used for ongoing actions that occur in the present.
  - Future: **will/shall* + *be being* + past participle are used for ongoing actions that occur in the future (*rarely used).

- **Passive perfect progressive/continuous tense:**
  - Past: **had* + *been being* + present participle are used for ongoing actions that occur before another in the past (*rarely used).
  - Present: **has/have* + *been being* + present participle are used for ongoing actions that occur before another in the present (*rarely used).
  - Future: **will have/shall have* + *been being* + past participle are used for ongoing actions that occur before another in the future (*rarely used).

Punctuation checklist

Indicating

- **Indicating possession**
  - Has an apostrophe followed by the letter *s* (*-'s*) been used to indicate possession by a singular entity or by plural entities whose nouns do not end in an *s*?
  - Where a possessing entity is plural and its noun is regular (that is, formed by adding *-s* or *-es*), does an apostrophe follow the *s* (*-s'* or *-es'*)?

- Where a noun ends in *y*, and its plural is created by replacing the *y* with *ies*, is the *s* followed by an apostrophe (-*ies'*)?
- Does possession by entities whose names end in an *s* take an apostrophe followed by *s* (-*'s*), except where the last syllable comprises more than one sibilant (a hissing sound) or where the name is a classical one ending in an *s*?

- **Indicating omitted letters, words, and phrases**
  - Have the types of omission shown in the left column below been indicated with the punctuation mark in the corresponding right column?

○ Omitted letter/s within words (contraction)	Apostrophe
○ Omitted letter/s within a word (substitution)	Em dash or two-em dash
○ Omitted letter/s at the end of words (abbreviation)	Period
○ Omitted word/s in parallel constructions (repetition ellipsis)	Comma or semicolon
○ Omitted word/s in a quotation (substitution ellipsis)	Ellipses (three successive points)

- **Indicating distancing, dialect and slang**
  - Have you used quotation marks to distance yourself, the writer, and the publisher from an assertion, to indicate the unusual usage of a term or that it is a misnomer, or to indicate that it is questionable?
  - Have you used quotation marks to indicate dialect or slang that contrasts with the register of the text?

- **Indicating quotations**
  - Have you used quotation marks to indicate direct speech and material taken from published texts?
  - For American English (AmE) style, have you used double quotation marks, with single quotation marks used for quotations within quotations?

- For British English (BrE) style, have you used single quotation marks with double quotation marks used for quotations within quotations?

- **Quotations of direct speech**
  - For AmE style, have commas that form part of the punctuation of a passage – not of the quoted words – been placed within the closing quotation mark?
  - For BrE, have commas been placed outside of the closing quotation mark if they do not form part of the quoted material, but inside, if they do?
  - For AmE, have terminating punctuation marks been placed within the closing quotation mark whether or not they form part of the quoted material?
  - For BrE, have terminating punctuation marks been placed within the closing quotation mark if they are part of the quoted material, but outside if they do not?

- **Quotations from published texts**
  - Have direct quotations of up to 100 words of material taken directly from published texts been enclosed in quotation marks?
  - Have the AmE and BrE conventions for single versus double quotation marks also been applied to quotations of published material?
  - For quotations that extend over more than one paragraph, has a quotation mark been placed at the beginning of every paragraph, with a closing quotation mark being placed only at the end of the quotation?
  - For quotations of more than 100 words, has the quotation been indented from the surrounding text, without quotation marks?

- **Titles of short works**
  - Have quotation marks been used to indicate the titles of short works such as the following?
    - Short poems
    - Short stories
    - Songs

- Have quotation marks been used to indicate parts of publications, such as the following?
  - Articles in journals
  - Chapters in books
- For AmE, have double quotation marks been used?
- For BrE, have single quotation marks been used?

- **Titles of published stand-alone works**
  - Have italics been used to indicate the titles of published stand-alone works such as the following?
    - Books
    - Catalogues
    - Epic poems
    - Newspapers
    - Periodicals
    - Pamphlets
    - Posters
    - Plays
    - Films
    - TV and radio series
    - Albums, CDs and DVDs

- **Names of craft and vehicles**
  - Have italics been used to indicate the names of craft and vehicles such as the following?
    - Aircraft
    - Motor vehicles
    - Ships
    - Trains

- **Indicating emphasis, highlighting and function**
  - Have italics been used to indicate emphasis or to highlight a text element, as determined by your style guide and style sheet?
  - As an alternative to italics, has bold been used to indicate emphasis or to highlight a text element, as determined by your style guide and style sheet?

- Have italics been used for particular predetermined purposes within your text, including the following?
  - To discuss a word, phrase, or term
  - To distinguish a particular function within a text, for example, the names of word classes in dictionaries
- Has bold been used for particular predetermined purposes within your text, including the following?
  - Headings
  - Headwords
  - New terms on first appearance that are explained further on in the text, or elsewhere, such as the glossary

- **Indicating foreign words and phrases**
  - Have italics been used to indicate foreign words and phrases that are still considered to be foreign, and not yet part of the English language?
  - Where you are uncertain about whether a particular word should be italicized, have you consulted the print version of a recently published reputable dictionary?

Demarcating

- **Demarcating initiating phrases**
  - Has a comma been used to demarcate initiating phrases (other than short initiating adverbial phrases where no misreading without the demarcating comma is possible) from the clause introduced?

- **Demarcating phrase lists in initiating position**
  - Have lists that precede the main independent clause been demarcated from the main independent clause with a colon or a dash?

- **Demarcating dependent/subordinate initiating clauses**
  - Where a dependent clause precedes an independent clause, has a comma been placed after the dependent clause?

- **Demarcating clause lists in initiating position**
  - Where a clause list precedes the main independent clause, has it been demarcated from the main independent clause with a colon or a dash?
- **Demarcating intervening phrases (which include single words)**
  - Where a phrase intervenes in a sentence, has it been demarcated with a pair of the most suitable of commas, dashes or parentheses?
  - Where an intervening phrase is short, has it been demarcated with a pair of commas?
  - Where an intervening phrase is emphasized, has it been demarcated with a pair of dashes?
  - Where an intervening phrase is not emphasized or is de-emphasized, has it been demarcated with a pair of commas?
  - Where an intervening phrase is an appositive, has it been demarcated with a pair of commas?
  - Where an intervening phrase is long, has it been demarcated with a pair of dashes?
  - Where an intervening phrase does not fit comfortably into the meaning and syntax of the main clause, has it been demarcated with a pair of dashes?
  - Where an intervening phrase is an unimportant point, has it been demarcated with a pair of parentheses?
  - Where an intervening phrase comprises an exception, has it been demarcated with a pair of parentheses?
  - Where an intervening phrase comprises a short list of examples, has it been demarcated with a pair of parentheses?
  - Where an intervening phrase comprises an acronym or a technical synonym, has it been demarcated with a pair of parentheses?
  - Where an intervening word is an abbreviation, has it been demarcated with a pair of parentheses?
  - Where an intervening phrase is a translation or a scientific name, has it been demarcated with a pair of parentheses?

- Where an intervening phrase is a cross-reference, has it been demarcated with a pair of parentheses?
- Where an intervening phrase is a numerical equivalent, has it been demarcated with a pair of parentheses?

- **Placement of intervening phrase demarcators**
  - Have pairs of phrase demarcating punctuation marks been placed so that they enclose only the intervening phrase?

- **Demarcating nested intervening phrase demarcators**
  - Where a primary intervening phrase is demarcated with commas, has the secondary, or nested, intervening phrase been demarcated with a pair of either of the two remaining options for demarcating intervening phrases: parentheses or dashes?

- **Demarcating intervening parenthetical clauses**
  - Have intervening parenthetical clauses been demarcated from the surrounding sentences with a pair of dashes or a pair of parentheses?
  - Have a pair of dashes been used where an intervening clause is emphasized?
  - Have a pair of dashes been used where an intervening clause is long?
  - Have a pair of dashes been used where an intervening clause does not fit comfortably into the meaning and syntax of the main clause; that is, it digresses from the development and sequencing of ideas?
  - Have a pair of parentheses been used to demarcate de-emphasized intervening parenthetical clauses?
  - Where there is only one intervening parenthetical clause or sentence, has the terminal punctuation mark been placed outside of the closing parenthesis, not within it?
  - Where parenthetical information consists of two sentences, has the first sentence been terminated with a terminal punctuation mark, while the second one has not?

- **Demarcating relative (dependent) clauses**
  - Have defining relative dependent clauses occurring within the independent clause been left undemarcated?
  - Have non-defining relative clauses been demarcated with a pair of commas from the surrounding independent clause?

- **Demarcating concluding parenthetical phrases**
  - Where a parenthetical phrase has been added at the end of a main independent clause, has a comma or dash been used to demarcate it from the independent clause, with a terminal punctuation mark (period, question mark, exclamation mark, or in the case of ellipsis, a dash or ellipsis points) used to terminate it?
  - Where parentheses have been used, does the terminating punctuation mark follow the closing parenthesis?

- **Demarcating concluding phrase lists**
  - When a list follows an independent clause, including when the initiating independent clause contains a phrase like 'the following', does a colon demarcate the list from the preceding independent clause?

- **Demarcating concluding parenthetical clauses**
  - Where a parenthetical clause has been added at the end of a main independent clause, has a comma or dash been used to demarcate it from the independent clause and a terminal punctuation mark (period, question mark, exclamation mark, or in the case of ellipsis, a dash or ellipsis points) been used to terminate it?
  - Where parentheses have been used, does the terminating punctuation mark follow the closing parenthesis?
  - Where parenthetical information consists of a two sentences, has the first sentence been terminated

with a terminal punctuation mark, while the second one has not?

- In instances where a sentence enclosed within parentheses is parenthetical within the context of the paragraph, not within a sentence, has the terminating punctuation mark been placed inside the closing parenthesis?

- **Demarcating concluding dependent clauses**
  - Where a defining dependent clause follows an independent clause, has it been left undemarcated from the preceding independent clause?
  - Where a non-defining dependent clause follows an independent clause, has a comma been used to demarcate the dependent clause from the independent clause?
  - Has each relative clause been double-checked to see that it has been punctuated to reflect whether it is defining or non-defining in meaning?

- **Demarcating concluding clause lists**
  - Where a list is preceded by an independent clause, and this clause contains a phrase like 'the following', has a colon been used to demarcate the list from the preceding clause?

Conjoining

- **Conjoined independent clauses**
  - Where independent clauses have been conjoined by a co-ordinating conjunction, has a comma preceding the conjunction been used to demarcate the first independent clause from the second independent clause, except where both clauses are short and where no misreading is possible?
  - Where independent clauses have been conjoined with an adverb (including a transitional adverb), does a semicolon precede the adverb demarcating the first independent clause from the second independent clause? Has the adverb preceding the subsequent

independent clause been demarcated from it with a comma, except after *thus* or *therefore* when the relationship described by the adverb is not emphasized?

- Where independent clauses have been conjoined without an adverb, has a semicolon been used to demarcate the first independent clause from the second independent clause where the relationship between them is neutral; that is, the subsequent independent clause involves no abrupt change in idea or tone and does not expand on or illustrate the preceding clause?
- Where independent clauses have been conjoined without an adverb, has a dash been used to demarcate the first independent clause from the second independent clause where the subsequent independent clause involves an abrupt change in notion or tone?
- Where independent clauses have been conjoined without an adverb, has a colon been used to demarcate them where the second independent clause expands on or illustrates the first?
- Where a colon has been used to demarcate conjoined independent clauses, has the capitalization of the word following the colon been applied in terms of the selected capitalization style (AmE, BrE or other)?
- Have commas been used to demarcate conjoined independent clauses from one another only where the following three criteria have been met: there are (1) three (2) short independent clauses that (3) have an identical subject?

Terminating

Have terminating punctuation marks been used to end all sentences, as specified below?

• Have periods been used to terminate statements (declarative sentences) and polite requests phrased as questions (imperative sentences)?

- Have periods been used to terminate sentences that include indirect questions and structures that include interrogative words, such as *why*?
- Have question marks been used to terminate direct questions?
- Have direct questions as the subjects of sentences been terminated with a question mark?
- Have exclamation marks been used to terminate statements (declarative sentences) and commands (imperative sentences) where emphasis is required or where strong emotion is involved?
- Have exclamation marks been used to terminate interjections and exclamations?
- Have exclamation marks been avoided to imply meanings that could have been conveyed by appropriate words, suitably arranged and punctuated?
- Have dashes been used to terminate sentences in dialogue where the speaker has been interrupted?
- Have ellipsis points been used to terminate sentences where the words or thoughts of a character or narrator trail off?

GLOSSARY

Adverbial: A functional clause element that modifies as an adverb, giving information about cause, degree, manner, space or time. Adverbials can be repositioned with some flexibility within the clause, and they can be removed altogether without making the clause ungrammatical.

Adverbial complement: Unlike an adverbial, an adverbial complement cannot be omitted without making a clause ungrammatical. It can have a linking (or copular) function, referring to the subject, or it can have a similar function in relation to the object. In both instances, it provides essential information about a subject or an object, making the clause or sentence in which it appears understandable and grammatical.

Agent: A person or thing acting on the object or being linked to the complement.

Agreement: The correspondence between words reflected in their form. Words can agree in grammatical case, gender, person and number. There are three factors that determine agreement, and these are attraction, form and notion – see related entries, below.

Agreement, attraction: Where the form of a word has been determined by the proximity of another – often on the basis of the form sounding correct to educated native speakers – the agreement has been determined by the principle of attraction. In terms of subject-verb agreement, this refers to the verb taking the form of the nearest subject or element of a subject. While this form of agreement is acceptable in spontaneous speech and informal writing, it is not acceptable in formal speech and writing.

Agreement, formal: Where the form of a word has been determined by the form of another, the agreement is formal. In terms of subject-verb agreement, this refers to the convention that a singular subject should take a singular verb and a plural subject should take a plural verb.

Agreement, notional: Where the form of a word has been determined by the notion – or meaning, rather than the form – of another, the agreement is notional. In terms of subject-verb agreement, this refers to the principle that the form of a verb can be determined by the meaning of the subject.

Antecedent: The preceding word, phrase or clause represented by a subsequently occurring pronoun.

Appositive: An appositive renames a term that it follows and sometimes that it precedes, specifying (defining) it, or acting as an equivalent (non-defining, or parenthetical) – see related entries, below.

Appositive, defining (or restrictive): When an appositive is defining, the meaning of the preceding or following term is specified, limited or restricted, and therefore, the defining (or restrictive) construction is not demarcated with a pair of demarcating punctuation marks.

Appositive, parenthetical (also non-defining or non-restrictive): When an appositive is parenthetical, and meaning is clarified, the parenthetical construction is demarcated with a pair of demarcating punctuation marks.

Case: The form that a noun or pronoun takes to show whether it is the subject (subjective case) or object (objective case) of a verb, or whether it shows possession (possessive case) of somebody or something.

Category/class, words and phrases, formal (or lexical): Words and phrases belong to different classes (also known as lexical categories, lexical classes, and parts of speech), referred to in this book as *word* and *phrase classes*. The number of word classes can vary between seven and nine, depending on the view of the linguist concerned.

The non-variable word classes are the following:

- adjective
- adverb
- conjunction
- noun
- preposition
- pronoun
- verb

The variable word classes are the following:

- articles (considered by some authors to be adjectives)
- interjection (considered by some authors to be a form of adverb)

The phrase classes are the following:

- adjective
- adverb
- genitive
- noun
- prepositional
- verb

Clause: A group of words that contains at least a subject and a verb, and is part of a sentence, or on its own comprises a simple sentence. A clause can be grammatically dependent or independent – see related entries, below.

Clause, dependent (or subordinate): When a clause is grammatically dependent, or subordinate, it cannot stand alone as a sentence but needs to be part of a grammatically independent sentence. It is made grammatically dependent on an independent clause by a preceding subordinating word or construction.

Clause, independent: When a clause is grammatically independent, it can stand alone as a sentence.

Complement: Where a word or words play the role of a predicate, completing the meaning of the subject, or where they complete the meaning of a predicate element such as an object or indirect object, the functional role is that of a complement.

Conjunction: A word used to connect, or conjoin, words, phrases and clauses – see related entries, below.

Conjunction, coordinating: A conjunction that connects words, phrases and clauses that have the same hierarchical grammatical status, for example, two independent clauses. The coordinating conjunctions are *and, but, for, or, nor, so* and *yet.*

Conjunction, subordinating: A conjunction that connects a clause of a lower grammatical status to one of a higher grammatical status, that is, a dependent (or subordinate) clause to an independent clause. Examples of subordinating conjunctions are *although, as, because, if, since, when* and *while.*

Construction: A syntactic group of words such as a phrase, a clause or a sentence – see related entries, below.

Construction, absolute: A phrase that – unlike a participial phrase used as an adjective, which needs something to modify – is not grammatically dependent on an element in another clause.

Construction, concluding (or final): A word, phrase or clause that follows the main clause of a sentence. If the concluding construction is parenthetical (also non-defining or non-restrictive), it is demarcated from the remainder of the sentence with a comma, a dash or a pair of parentheses; if it is defining (or restrictive), it is not demarcated from the remainder of the sentence.

Construction, conjoining: A word together with one or more punctuation marks, such as a comma preceding a coordinating conjunction used to join independent clauses. Certain punctuation marks on their own may also be used to conjoin independent clauses.

Construction, defining (or restrictive): A construction is defining when it is essential to the meaning and grammaticality of the clause or sentence in which it appears; thus, it could not be deleted without the meaning of the clause or sentence changing.

Construction, initiating (or initial): A word, phrase or clause that comes before the main clause of a sentence. An initiating construction is usually demarcated from the remainder of the sentence with a comma, but there are instances where the demarcating punctuation mark is optional, and where it is optional, it may not be desirable.

Construction, intervening (or internal): A word, phrase or clause that is within, or intervenes in, the main clause of a sentence. An intervening construction is demarcated from the remainder of the sentence with a pair of commas, a pair of parentheses or a pair of dashes if it is non-defining; it is not demarcated if it is defining.

Construction, parenthetical (also non-defining or non-restrictive): When a construction is not essential to the meaning and grammaticality of the sentence as a whole, that is, it could be deleted from the sentence without changing its meaning, the construction is parenthetical (also non-defining or non-restrictive).

Derivation: The formation of new words from existing words by adding or removing parts of the word, such as an affix. The change can involve a change in word class or a switch from negative to positive, among others – also see *Inflection*, below.

Ellipsis: The omission of a word or construction where not doing this would involve repeating information that could easily and unambiguously be filled in by a reader.

En dash (also *en rule*): The en dash is used predominantly as the demarcating dash (one of the three demarcators – comma, dash, parentheses). It does have other uses too, such as, substituting for *to* in ranges and, like the virgule, or solidus (slash), giving an alternative. These latter uses of the dash may vary for American English (AmE) style and British English (BrE) style, and even within these major groupings, so do consult your style guide.

Grammar: The study of the structural relationships in a language and the conventions that apply to these. In this book, grammar is referred to as *language structuring.*

Grammatical/grammaticality: Conforming to the conventions for relating syntactic units to one another.

Grammatical dependence: A condition that exists when a word or group of words lacking a subject or finite verb, or preceded by a subordinating conjunction necessitates linking it to another grammatically independent construction.

Grammatical form: Grammatical form refers to the types of words, phrases and clauses that can be used as any of the functional elements within clauses, that is, the form that the functional elements can take.

Grammatical function: Grammatical function refers to the function that words, phrases and clauses perform in clauses. The functional classes are subject, object, predicator (or verb), object (direct and indirect), complement, adverbial complement and adverbial.

Grammatical independence: A group of words that has at least a subject and a finite verb and no other word or group of words that makes it dependent on another group of words.

Inflection: The formation of grammatical variants of the same words by adding or removing parts of the word, such as an affix. It can also involve an internal change in spelling. The change may involve a change in grammatical category, such a change in case, gender, person or number, among others – also see *Derivation*, above.

Misreading: A misunderstanding or misinterpretation resulting in the reader having to backtrack and reread the part of the text that was misunderstood or misinterpreted. Misreadings are often caused by faulty syntax and punctuation as well as poor diction, or choices of words.

Morpheme: The smallest meaningful part of a word, such as the prefix *pre-*.

Object: The functional element of a clause – which could be a word, a phrase or a clause – that is affected by a verb or a preposition.

Paragraph: The subdivision of a text into thematic, topical or subject groups. Thus each paragraph deals with a particular aspect, or area, of the larger containing text.

Parallel/Parallelism: The similar content and function of elements of sentences and paragraphs – including elements in a series – that are reflected in their similar grammatical form, or structure.

Participle: A form of verb that is used as an adjective and in compound tenses (perfect and progressive, or continuous) of verbs. Be aware that while certain words may have the form of a present or past participle, they could be ordinary adjectives or gerunds – see related entries, below.

Participle, past: A participle that ends in *-ed* with regular verbs, but that with irregularly formed verbs, involves an internal change in spelling, which may or may not be the same as the past tense form.

Participle, present: A participle that ends in *-ing*.

Phrase: A syntactic unit consisting of a meaningful sequence of two or more words that together contribute to the meaning of a clause or sentence. Linguists and grammarians often use the term *phrase* to refer to a single word when the same conventions and terms that would apply to a phrase also apply to a single word.

Predicate: The part of the sentence other than the subject, or sentence element that is acting as the subject, which includes either only the verb or the verb and all the remaining, or subsequent, sentence elements.

Sentence: A group of words that begins with a capital letter and ends with a terminal punctuation mark, and which contains at least one independent clause – see related entries, below.

Sentence, complex: A sentence that has at least one dependent clause.

Sentence, compound: A sentence consisting of two or more independent clauses.

Sentence, compound-complex: A sentence that consists of at least two independent clauses, one of which is modified by a dependent clause.

Sentence, simple: A sentence consisting of only one independent clause.

Sentence fragment: A group of words that begins with a capital letter and ends with a terminal punctuation mark but that does not contain at least one independent clause, and is therefore not independent. Sentence fragments are acceptable only for justifiable stylistic reasons.

Stylistic: The use of language to achieve a specific, justifiable meaning and effect.

Subject: In an active sentence, the part of the sentence that is the doer of the action expressed by the verb; in a passive sentence, it is the recipient of the action expressed by the verb.

Syntactic unit: A group of words within a sentence.

Syntax: The grammatical arrangement of words, phrases and clauses.

Text: Any written work, which could be a poem, an essay, a novel, a report, among others.

Verb (or predicator): A word or phrase that denotes action or a state of being – see related entries, below.

Verb, base form: The infinitive form without the preceding *to*. This is the form that main entries in dictionaries take.

Verb, infinitive: The base form with the preceding *to*. Infinitives function as nouns, adjectives and adverbs.

Verb, intransitive: A verb or verb construction that does not require an object to make the clause in which it appears complete and grammatical.

Verb, irregular: A verb whose past tense is not formed by adding *-ed* to the base form. Its past tense and past participle may not be the same, and its third person present tense may involve a further internal change in spelling.

Verb, linking (or copula): A type of intransitive verb or verb construction that links the subject to, or identifies it with, a complement. The verb *be* is the most prevalent linking, or copular, verb.

Verb, regular: A verb whose past tense is formed by adding *-ed* to the base form. The past tense and past participle forms of regular verbs are the same. Their third person present tense is formed by adding *s*.

Verb, transitive: A verb or verb construction that requires an object to make the clause in which it appears complete and grammatical. This type of verb conveys the action from the subject to the object.

Verbal: A group of words that are formed from verbs, comprising infinitives, gerunds and participles. Verbals function as nouns, adjectives and adverbs.

SELECTED BIBLIOGRAPHY

Du Toit, P., Heese, M. & Orr, M., 2006. *Practical Guide to Reading, Thinking and Writing Skills.* Cape Town: Oxford University Press Southern Africa.

Einsohn, A., 2000. *The Copyeditor's Handbook.* Berkeley: University of California Press.

HarperCollins Publishers, 1990. *Collins Cobuild English Grammar.* 1st ed. Glasgow: HarperCollins Publishers.

Johnson, E. D., 1991. *The Handbook of Good English.* New York: Washington Square Press.

Leech, G., Deuchar, M. & Hoogenraad, R., 1985. *English Grammar for Today.* Basingstoke: Macmillan.

Oxford University Press, 2005. *New Hart's Rules.* New York: Oxford University Press.

Pascal, E., 1994. *Jung to Live by.* London: Souvenir Press.

Todd, L., 2001. *Cassell's Guide to Punctuation.* London: Cassell.

INDEX

162